THE FUTURE OF HUMANITY: RACING TOWARD ETERNITY

Pastor Robert Taylor

The Future of Humanity:
Racing Toward Eternity

Written by Pastor Robert Taylor

Edition 2017

Copyright 2017 Robert Taylor

ISBN 13: 978-0692831663

For permission requests, write to the publisher, addressed "Attention: Permissions Coordinator," at the address below.

Robert Taylor
roberttaylor699@yahoo.com

Unless otherwise noted, all scripture references are from the New American Standard Version of the Bible.

Editing & Formatting: Lorraine Castle –
Castle Virtual Solutions LLC
http://www.castlevirtualsolutions.com/

Dedication Page

This book is dedicated to my Lord and Savior, Christ Jesus!
I consider being chosen for salvation a very precious thing
and it's because of what Jesus did for me on the cross,
everything I am, I owe to Him. The truths I set forth in this
book results from the wisdom and insight that the Lord
gives. My desire to write and bring glory to Him is a great
honor.

Foreword

I met Robert Taylor in the sixties when my family moved across the street from his family in Philadelphia, PA. The strongest memory I have of Robert and his family is the way that they embraced my family with love even though we were strangers. Theirs was a home full of children, love and activity. In the summer, I would spend hours sitting on their front porch. Robert was closer in age to my younger brother and I was closer in age to Robert's older sister. It was a perfect connection. As happens so often, as we grew into adulthood, we each made career decisions that took us down different paths.

Fast forward 20+ years and Robert and I reconnected on social media. Robert is a Pastor in North Carolina and I'm an editor and book publisher in New Jersey. To state an over-used cliché, it truly is a small world and social media has made the world even smaller!

I didn't hesitate when Robert asked me to assist in publishing his book. In his debut book, **"The Future of Humanity: Racing Toward Eternity,"** Robert answers questions that many Christians may have about the end times. Led by the Holy Spirit, Pastor Robert analyzes the books of The Bible that refer to the end times connecting the predictions referenced in The Bible and connecting those references to our Christian walk today. In **"The Future of Humanity: Racing Toward Eternity,"** we are reminded that we do not have to go to others for answers to our concerns. Your answers are right there in The Bible – the best-selling book of all time! **"The Future of Humanity: Racing Toward Eternity"** should be required reading for the churched and unchurched. Not only does it clear up the mystery of the end times, it will relieve the fears that some Christians may have concerning the end times.

Instead of gloom, doom and harsh judgment, Robert describes the Joy of walking with the Lord and learning more about Him and His intentions toward us. Robert eloquently states, "For the Christ follower, realizing that the Lord could step through the door and appear for them at any moment, is designed to bring comfort and encouragement as well as motivation for Christlikeness!" We are reminded that in Christ Jesus, there is no condemnation when Robert writes, "…Christ followers will never be condemned!" After reading this book, the reader is encouraged, illuminated and energized to draw closer to God as He draws closer to us.

Pastor Robert studied at Temple University (Philadelphia, PA), Rhema Bible Training College (Broken Arrow, OK) and Southern Illinois University (Carbondale, IL). Robert is the Pastor of Teach Well Bible Church.

Lorraine M. Castle
Author of "The Altar Will Alter You"
Owner of Castle Virtual Solutions LLC

Acknowledgments

I would like to express my very great appreciation to my wife, Toleto Taylor, for her continued encouragement as well as her help in typing the manuscript. She's a tremendous blessing to me. I would like to offer my special thanks to Lorraine Castle and her company, Castle Virtual Solutions, for her dedicated and professional efforts of helping to bring this book to fruition. I'm particularly grateful for the foreword that Lorraine wrote. I would like to thank all who have supported the teaching ministry of Teach Well Bible Church, as this book is an outreach of the ministry.

Preface

"He who will not look forward must look behind"
(Illustrated World of Proverbs) Gaelic Proverb [16919]

This book is a study of what the Bible says is going to take place in the future. Only the Bible can predict future events with 100 percent accuracy. Let's consider a few of some of the world's worst predictions. King George II said in 1773 the American colonies had little stomach for revolution. How did that work out? An official of the White Star Line, speaking of the Titanic, which launched in 1912, declared that the ship was unsinkable. We saw how that worked out! In 1939, the New York Times said the problem with TV was that people had to glue their eyes to a screen, and that the average American wouldn't have time for it (The World's Worst Predictions in *Reader's Digest*, March 1991). We know how all those predictions turned out!

The word used to describe these future events is eschatology. Eschatology means the "teachings about the end times." It deals with the end of human history and human existence as we know it. Eschatology refers to the events that are foretold to happen, both in relation to the individual as well as to the world. We must understand that from a biblical perspective, history is not cyclical, but linear (following in a logical or sequential pattern). **This means that history is advancing, racing towards a goal. God is controlling and driving history towards the fulfillment of His divine purposes for humanity.** The focus of the book, "The Future of Humanity: Racing Toward Eternity," is to bring an awareness of God's calendar of events for the end of time! This book will survey and focus on key topics related to future events.

Reasons to Read This Book:

1.   More than 25 percent of the Bible is dedicated to prophecy (eschatology). J. Barton Payne's Encyclopedia of Biblical Prophecy lists 1,239 prophecies in the Old Testament and 578 prophecies in the New Testament for a total of 1,817. These encompass 8,352 verses out of 31,102 verses which is more than 25 percent! There are many reasons why so much of the Bible is dedicated to prophetic (future) events, but in the end, there's only one purpose: to point the attention of humanity to Jesus Christ. Apostle John said it best with these words, **"For the testimony of Jesus is the spirit of prophecy" (Revelation 19:10, NASB).**

2.   Previously fulfilled prophecies point to unprecedented credibility to the Scriptures' claim of being the Word of God!

3.   The study of Bible prophecy is a very important aspect of proper Christian living. Apostle Paul said, **"All Scripture is inspired by God and is profitable for teaching, for reproof, for correction, for training in righteousness; so that the man of God may be adequate, equipped for every good work" (2 Timothy 3:16).** The term **"All Scripture"** includes Bible prophecy, which means that it's profitable for teaching, for reproof, for correction, for training in righteousness! Robert L. Deffinbaugh remarks, "The Bible contains a great deal of prophecy, and the study of biblical prophecy is a matter of great importance. God's plans for the future and His promised blessings are the basis for our hope and the motivation for our endurance, even in the midst of great adversity or affliction. People feel strongly about the things which matter most, and prophecy is rightly perceived to be a subject of great import to all men. Since

our eternal destiny is intertwined with the prophecies of the Word of God, we should have strong feelings about prophecy," (God's Plan for the Future).

4.   The topics discussed in this book are a call to every Christ follower into a more intimate relationship with God through Jesus Christ. For those who are not following Christ, this book can help you to see your need for Christ as the Lord and Savior of your life.

5.   When properly understood, and embraced, the topics covered in this book infuse joy into your life as well as hope for the future.

6.   The Christ follower's life should be lived with an earnest expectation that God is in control of all of life in the present and beyond. Understanding and embracing the topics in this book brings stability to our faith and challenges us to remain faithful to Christ no matter the circumstances.

7.   The topics discussed in this book encourage godly living. We are to understand, that in the end, committed study of biblical prophecy is a continuous reminder of the awesome power of God, the wonderful glory of Jesus Christ, and the absolute certainty that promises for the future will come to pass. This brings forth many Christ like characteristics in the life of the Christ follower, a fact attested to by apostle Paul. He said, **"For the grace of God has appeared, bringing salvation to all men, instructing us to deny ungodliness and worldly desires and to live sensibly, righteously and godly in this present age, looking for the blessed hope and the appearing of the glory of our great God and Savior, Christ Jesus" (Titus 2:11-13).** Notice that godliness is connected to looking for the blessed hope and appearing of our great God and Savior, Christ Jesus!

8. For some reason, the most credible source of information on future events, God's Word, continues to escape notice. However, no other source of knowledge on future events is backed by the tons of historical data, archaeological proof, as well as the overwhelming mathematical probability of their fulfillment.

9. The very definition of God includes His unique ability to see and know from the distant past to the distant future, declaring the end from the beginning. God alone can foresee world events with 100-percent accuracy thousands of years in advance. Unlike other religious texts that claim divine origin, the Word of God can point to its unprecedented track record in foreseeing the future. This is because the Word of God is not the product of man's imagination, but rather the testimony of godly men who were carried along by the power of the Holy Spirit to speak from God. Prophecy that's come to pass authenticates the Word of God, proving it to be from God. Knowing about future events deserves our attention. Finally, I believe the reading of this book will challenge and humble you. Being a part of humanity, this book is for you! Be encouraged!

Contents

Chapter One: Behold, The Bridegroom is Coming!

This is a very important promise regarding the Pretribulation Rapture of the church. This promise is found in the gospel of John 14:2-3. It's a promise that the Lord Jesus gave while gathered with His apostles in an upper room on the evening before His crucifixion, see Luke 22:7-14. It was through this promise that Jesus purposed to encourage and calm the troubled hearts of His closest followers. See John 14:1. The question becomes, why were His followers troubled? On the one hand, these men had committed themselves to the belief that Jesus was the Messiah who was promised; the one who'd destroy the forces of evil and restore the kingdom of God to the earth (Matthew 16:16). Because of this commitment, they had left their means of living to follow Jesus (Matthew 4:18-22; 9:9) and had obeyed His commission to proclaim to Israel that the kingdom of God was at hand (Matthew 10:1-7; Luke 9:1-2). These men were fully persuaded that Jesus would restore the kingdom of God on earth while they were still alive (Acts 1:6) and that He'd remain on the earth as the King of kings to rule over that kingdom. However, on the other hand, Jesus had already said to them that He would ascend to heaven (John 6:62; 12:35-36; 13:33). As a matter of fact, the passage in John 13:33 caused Peter to ask the Lord where He was going (John 13:36), and Jesus said, **"Where I go, you cannot follow Me now; but you will follow Me later" (John 13:36).** Peter asked why he could not follow Jesus in John 13:37. We must understand that Peter's responses show that the Lord's statements brought about troubling questions among the apostles. In other words, if the Lord would be with them for only a little while longer and then would leave for a place to which they could not go for an undisclosed amount of time, did this mean that Jesus would not bring the rule of God while they were still alive? What implications would Jesus' leaving have, with respect to His remaining on earth to rule God's kingdom? What effect would Jesus' departure have on the entire kingdom program? Why does He have leave? How would the Lord's leaving affect them? These are but some of the reasons why their hearts would be troubled!

The Promise Examined

We'll start by first looking at some of the introductory statements that are before the promise. They are recorded for us in John 14:2. **"In My Father's house are many dwelling places."** The word **"dwelling places"** was used for a place where a traveler can stay at the end of a day's journey! It reminds Christ followers of the fact that this present world is not our home! For that reason, the Bible calls us **"strangers and exiles on the earth" (Hebrews 11:13), "aliens and strangers" (1 Peter 2:11)** because our citizenship is in heaven, at the Father's house! The Father's house is the lodging that's been secured for us at the end of our journey for this life! The Lord Jesus Christ has secured the lodging for us! We know that the Word of God teaches that God's place of dwelling is in heaven (Psalm 33:13-14; Isaiah 63:15; Deuteronomy 26:15; Psalm 80:14; Matthew 6:1,9). In other words, the Father's house is God's heavenly abode! The Father's house is the place to which Jesus is going and in which His people are also **promised a place!**

Jesus said that there are **"many"** dwelling places in the Father's house. The Father's house is a huge place that's large enough to give residence to as many as the Lord **calls!** In other words, there's room for the entire called out ones, the church, to dwell in the Father's house in heaven at the end of its present earthly journey! Praise God forevermore! Jesus said, **"if it were not so, I would have told you."** Our Lord said these words to confirm the truthfulness of His claim that there are many dwelling places in the Father's house! He also said, **"for I go to prepare a place for you."** Our Lord said these words to confirm the truthfulness of His claim that there are many dwelling places in the Father's house! He also said, **"for I go to prepare a place for you."** Our Lord is indicating that He would leave the apostles and go somewhere. When Jesus spoke these words, He was referring to His ascension to the Father in heaven. The word translated **"go"** in the Lord's statement **"I go"** is used for His ascension in Acts 1:10-11 and 1 Peter 3:22. Our Lord wanted to assure His apostles that His going to the Father's house was to prepare a place for them. Remember, that their hearts were troubled when He spoke of leaving them; now He is assuring them that His going away is for their advantage. We must be excited about this advantage!

The Lord is leaving to get a place ready for them and, having done that, He will come back and take them there! Jesus' going to prepare a place implied His return to take them there to be occupants of that place!

The Promise

The promise of the Lord is found in John 14:3. It reads, "**I will come again, and receive you to Myself.**" Having already spoken about going to the Father's house to prepare a place for them there, the Lord gave a conditional clause to emphasize the certainty of His coming to receive His apostles! In other words, His leaving would not be a permanent thing. It would set the stage for a wonderfully, glorious reunion! What an awesome promise we have from the Lord Jesus Christ! Now, let's examine the part of the promise that says, **"I will come again."** There's nothing stronger than a promise from the Lord containing the words **"I will."** We can count on it! Jesus is making the promise of His coming a very confident assertion! In other words, the Lord is assuring to us that His coming for us is certain! **Let there be no doubt about His coming; it'll certainly take place!** Are we looking for it? Are we confidently expecting it to happen? Are we excited about it taking place? I don't know about you, but I certainly am! Praise God forevermore! **"And receive you to Myself."** The word **"receive"** means **"to take to oneself, take along with."** The Lord is promising, **"I will take you to myself with Me to my Father's house!"** In Strong's Exhaustive Concordance of The Bible, page 3884, one of the root words for the verb **"receive"** is **"to take charge of."** Recall that Jesus told His apostles that after He went to His Father in heaven, He would send to them **"another Comforter,"** the Holy spirit, who would care for them (John 14:16-17; 16:7-15). In other words, while the Lord Jesus Christ is in heaven at the Father's house, the Holy Spirit has the oversight and **"charge of"** Jesus' followers on the earth. What an awesome thing it is to yield to the oversight of the Holy Spirit! But when Jesus returns for His church, He'll take **"charge of"** their care from the Holy Spirit! When the Lord told His apostles that **"I will come again,"** He made it very clear that He, not anyone else, would return and receive His followers, and that He would receive them to Himself! **This is because His return to receive His followers is very important to Him personally and that He's not entrusting this activity to anyone else!** Our Lord will not send for the church, but come in person to take us to the Father's house! How special is that? Paul emphasizes the same thing in his letter to the Christ followers at Thessalonica when he said, **"For the Lord Himself will descend from heaven" (1 Thessalonians 4:16).** How precious is that? The Word of God teaches that this return is important to the Lord on a personal level because it involves receiving His beloved bride, the church! **The Bridegroom is coming for His bride!** Listen to the words of Paul to the Christ followers at Corinth, **"For I am jealous for you with a godly jealousy; for I betrothed you to one husband, so that to Christ I might present you as a pure virgin" (2 Corinthians 11:2).** The word translated **"receive"** in the Lord's promise is used in describing the action of a bridegroom **"taking"** his betrothed wife unto himself. See Matthew 1:20, 24, where the same language is used for Joseph and Mary. Since that is the case, then one would conclude that, in the Lord's promise in John 14:3, **our Lord was giving an analogy between Jewish marriage customs in biblical times and His return to receive the church, His bride. We'll explore that analogy later in this chapter.** The last part of the promise is found in the latter part of John 14:3. It reads, **"that where I am, you may be also."** This statement gives us the purpose of Jesus' coming to receive His church. Note that the Lord did not say that His coming to receive His church was that He could be where they are, which is on the earth. No, He said that His purpose was so the church can be where He is, which is in heaven at the father's house. Praise the Lord

God forevermore! **The church is going to be taken up away from the earth in order to be with Jesus in heaven! What a flight that will be!** Jesus' separation from His church is only temporary! Remember, Jesus shared this promise with His followers because their hearts were troubled and afraid. What an encouragement and a comfort this was to calm their troubled hearts. What about you and I who are Christ followers? It should encourage us as well! It should comfort us as well!

The reality of going to the Father's house can help guard our hearts from being afraid or troubled. No matter how badly things may be going in your life today, our Lord has given us a significant promise that's designed to alleviate or relieve the troubled heart! He's promised a wonderfully glorious future that involves being with Him in the Father's house! We have to focus on the place of our future dwelling which is the Father's house. The things that cause anxiety and fear in this life are not present in the Father's house. In Colossians 3:1-2, Paul reminds us to **"keep seeking the things above, where Christ is"** and to **"Set your mind on the things above."** According to John 14:2-3, the Father's house qualifies as the things above, **where Christ is!** Living in a fallen world can be very difficult at times. Living as Christ followers with a sin nature can be difficult at times. However, there's relief for the Christ follower due to the fact that our Lord Jesus Christ is going to remove us from this fallen world and take us with Him to the Father's house!

The Future-Coming View

Let's examine further lines of proof that the John 14:3 coming of Jesus is referring to a specific event of the future called the rapture! The future-coming view says that at one specific point in the future, the Lord Himself will descend from His Father's house (heaven) and remove His followers as an entire group from the earth to the Father's house to dwell with Him there.

1. The careful exegesis of John 14:2-3 which we've already covered supports this view. The future-coming view agrees with every feature of that exegesis.

2. The relationship of John 14:2-3 to the passage in 1 Thessalonians 4:13-18 is remarkable. The comparison of these two passages shows that they're identical to each other in many significant areas. **First,** as we've seen earlier, Jesus' coming again (John 14:3) involves a descending from heaven by the Lord Himself. This corresponds with **"the Lord Himself shall descend from heaven"** (1 Thessalonians 4:16). In other words, both passages present a coming in which the Lord Himself will descend from heaven. **Second,** as with the Lord's (John 14:3) coming, Jesus will receive His followers to Himself. In other words, the careful exegesis of John 14:3 indicates that along with the Lord's descent from heaven, Christ followers will be moved from the earth to meet Him. Corresponding with this, 1 Thessalonians 4:17 shows that along with the Lord's descent from heaven (v 16), Christ followers **"will be caught up together with them in the clouds to meet the Lord in the air"** (v 17). Both passages show a coming of the Lord that involves a movement of Christ followers from the earth to meet the Lord, i.e., a receiving of His followers to Himself. **Next,** we see that the purpose of the John 14:3 coming is that Christ followers can be with the Lord where He is. In harmony with this, 1 Thessalonians 4:17, says that the purpose of the Lord's descent from heaven is **"so we shall always be with the**

Lord." In other words, both passages deal with a coming of the Lord involving all Christ followers being with Him. Also, we've seen that the teaching of John 14:2-3 was given to Jesus' followers to calm afraid and troubled hearts (v 1). In the same way, the teaching of Paul in 1Thessalonians 4:13-18 was given to encourage and comfort hearts that were sorrowful (v 13-18). In other words, both passages present a return of Jesus involving truths that are designed to alleviate the troubled hearts of Christ followers. **These parallels of John 14:2-3 and 1 Thessalonians 4:13-18 leads to the conclusion that both passages refer to the same return of Jesus!**

It should be apparent that the relationship of John 14:2-3 to that of 1 Thessalonians 4:13-18 brings forth the conclusion that both passages are in reference to the identical return of the Lord for His church! They both speak about and teach of the rapture of the church!

3. A look at the Jewish Wedding Customs Analogy. Earlier in our chapter, we saw that in the promise of John 14:3, the Lord's words implied an analogy between Jewish wedding customs in biblical times and His return to receive His bride, the church. **This analogy is another strong proof for the future-coming view.**

Let's begin to examine this analogy. Although various sources describing the practice of Jewish marriage at the time of Jesus Christ differ in details, there's general agreement concerning its major elements. Jewish marriages included several steps: **first,** betrothal (which involved the prospective groom's traveling from his father's house to the home of the prospective bride, paying the purchase price, and thus establishing the marriage covenant); **second,** the groom's returning to his father's house (which meant remaining separate from his bride for 12 months, during which time, he prepared the living accommodations for his wife in his father's house); **third,** the groom's coming for his bride at a time not known exactly to her; **fourth,** his return with her to the groom's father's house to consummate the marriage and to celebrate the wedding feast for the next seven days (during which the bride remained closeted in her bridal chamber). In the Marriage of the Lamb all four of these steps of the Jewish wedding ceremony are evident!

The Jewish Wedding Analogy Summarized

1. Marriage Covenant. The father pays for the bride and establishes the marriage covenant (Acts 20:28; 1 Corinthians 6:19-20; 11:25; Ephesians 5:25-27). (Betrothal – 2 Corinthians 11:2).

2. Bridal Chamber Prepared. The son returns to his father's house and prepares the bridal chamber (John 6:62; 14:2; Acts 1:9-11).

3. Bride Fetched. At a time determined by the father, the groom fetches the bride to bring her to his father's house. Although the bride was expecting her groom to come for her, she did not know the time of his coming. As a result, the groom's arrival was preceded by a shout, which forewarned the bride to be prepared for his coming. (John 14:3; 1 Thessalonians 4:14-18). His return for her was imminent (at any moment).

4. Bride Cleansed. The bride undergoes ritual cleansing prior to the wedding ceremony (1 Corinthians 3:12-15; Revelation 19:7-8).

5. Wedding Ceremony. The private wedding ceremony (Revelation 19:7).

6. Consummation. In the privacy of the bridal chamber the bride and groom consummates the marriage (Revelation 19:7).

7. Marriage Feast. The celebratory marriage feast to which many are invited (Matthew 22:1-14; 25:1-13; Luke 12:36).

Just as the Jewish bridegroom took the initiative in marriage by leaving his father's house and traveling to the home of the prospective bride, so Jesus left His Father's house in heaven and traveled to the earth, the home of His prospective, the church, approximately two thousand years ago. In the same manner that the Jewish bridegroom came to the bride's home to obtain her by establishing a marriage covenant, so Jesus came to the earth to obtain the church by establishing a covenant. On the same night in which Jesus made his John 14:3 promise, He instituted communion. See 1 Corinthians 11:25. By shedding His blood on the cross the next day, He established a new covenant through which He obtained His church. Parallel to the custom of the Jewish bridegroom paying a purchase price by which he established the marriage covenant and through which he obtained his bride, Jesus paid a purchase price by which He established the new covenant and through which He obtained the church. The price He paid was the shedding of His own life blood. Paul shared 1 Corinthians 6:19-20 with the church at Corinth because of that purchase price. Just as the Jewish bride was declared set apart exclusively for her groom once the marriage covenant was established, so the church has been declared set apart exclusively for Christ (Ephesians 5:25-27; 1 Corinthians 1:2; 6:11;

Hebrews 10:10; 13:12; James 4:4; 1 John 2:15-16; 1 Thessalonians 4:3).

Just as the Jewish groom left the home of his bride and returned to his father's house after the marriage covenant had been established, so on the day of His ascension, Jesus left the earth, the home of the church, and returned to His Father's house in heaven after He established the new covenant and risen from the dead (John 6:62; Acts 1:9-11). As the Jewish groom remained separated from his bride in his father's house for a period of time after he left her home; so Christ has remained separated from the church in His Father's house for approximately 2000 years since He left the earth. The church is now living in that period of separation between the time of His departure and the time of His return. Parallel to the custom of the Jewish groom's preparing a dwelling place for his bride in his father's house during the time of separation, Jesus has been preparing a dwelling place for the church in His Father's house during the time of separation. Jesus stated that was the reason for Him going back to heaven. In the same manner as the Jewish groom came to take his bride to live with him at the end of the period of separation, so the Lord will come to take the church to live with Him at the end of His present period of separation from it (John 14:3).

Chapter Two: Distinguishing Between the Rapture of the Church and the Coming of Jesus

The rapture of the church and the second coming of Jesus with His holy angels are shown to be **two distinct events, thus they must take place at two different times!** Scripture shows that they're two different and unrelated programs of God. The Word of God teaches that the order of events which takes place at the rapture of the church will be the complete opposite of the order of events at the second coming of the Lord Jesus Christ. As we have seen in the chapter, **"Behold, The Bridegroom Is Coming,"** John 14:2-3 and 1 Thessalonians 4:13-18 both refer to the same coming of Jesus, and since Jesus' coming in 1 Thessalonians 4 is the coming to rapture the church from the earth, His coming in John 14:2-3 is also the coming to rapture the church from the earth! **While the rapture of the church is taking place, all unbelievers will be left on the earth to enter the next period of history. However, the reverse of this is true concerning the second coming of Jesus with His holy angels. The Bible indicates that at the coming of Jesus with His angels, all unbelievers will be removed from the earth in judgment, but the believers (not the church) will be left on the earth to enter the 1000 year reign (millennial kingdom) of the Lord Jesus Christ!** In other words, at the rapture, all Christ followers (the church) will be removed from the earth, but at the second coming of Jesus with His angels, all unbelievers will be removed from the earth! Only believers will enter

24

into the millennial kingdom of the Lord Jesus Christ. These are the believers who are left on the earth after the removal of all unbelievers at the second coming of Jesus with His angels!

Let's examine some lines of evidence concerning the opposite/reverse order teaching.

Line of evidence: Jesus' Teaching On The Parable Of The Wheat And The Tares.

Our passage of Scripture is found in Matthew 13:24-30. In this passage, Jesus taught this parable about the kingdom of heaven. It reads, **Jesus presented another parable to them, saying, "The kingdom of heaven may be compared to a man who sowed good seed in his field. But while his men were sleeping, his enemy came and sowed tares among the wheat, and went away. But when the wheat sprouted and bore grain, then the tares became evident also. The slaves of the landowner came and said to him, 'Sir, did you not sow good seed in your field? How then does it have tares?' And he said to them, 'An enemy has done this!' The slaves said to him, 'Do you want us then to go and gather them up?' But he said, 'No; for while you are gathering up the tares, you may uproot the wheat with them. Allow them both to grow together until the harvest; and in the time of harvest I will say to the reapers, "First gather up the tares and bind them in bundles to burn them up; but gather the wheat into my barn."** The Lord's interpretation of the parable is found in Matthew 13:36-43. In the Lord's interpretation, He gives us the following: **The farmer is the Son of Man (Jesus); the field is the world; the wheat are believers in the kingdom; the enemy is Satan; the tares are unbelievers; the harvest is the end of the world (the end of the age); the reapers are Jesus' angels.** After giving us the players of this event, the

Lord gives the order of the events. The tares will be **taken away** and destroyed first, and the wheat is **left behind** to be gathered into the barn. Jesus is teaching that when He sends forth His angels at the end of the age, they will gather out of the earth **"all"** unbelievers and cast them into a furnace of fire (41-42). In other words, we see that when Jesus taught about the wheat and the tares, He taught the following: When the Lord sends forth His angels at the end of the age, they will' separate all unbelievers from association with the kingdom by removing them from the earth in judgment! Once this is done, the believers (not the church) will be left on the earth to continue functioning in His kingdom! So, the believers that are alive when the Lord sends forth His angels will be left (not taken as some teach) to operate in His kingdom! We must be able to carefully interpret the parable of the wheat and the tares! When that's done, we come to the conclusion that our Lord is not teaching on the rapture of the church, but the removal of unbelievers from the earth!

Line Of Evidence: Jesus' Teaching On The Parable Of The Dragnet

Our passage Scripture is found in Matthew 13:47-50. In this passage, the Lord taught the parable concerning the kingdom of heaven. It reads, **"Again, the kingdom of heaven is like a dragnet cast into the sea, and gathering fish of every kind; and when it was filled, they drew it up on the beach; and they sat down and gathered the good fish into containers, but the bad they threw away. So it will be at the end of the age; the angels will come forth and take out the wicked from among the righteous, and will throw them into the furnace of fire; in that place there will be weeping and gnashing of teeth."**

In the Lord's interpretation of this parable, Jesus said that when the angels come forth during the end of the age, the wicked, not the righteous will be removed (taken out). The Lord also said that when the wicked are removed, they'll be taken out "from among the righteous." These two events (the wicked being removed and taken out from among the righteous) show that the righteous will be left on the earth when the wicked are taken away! Next, we see that when the wicked are removed, they'll be thrown into a terrible place of torment, (weeping, and gnashing of teeth). So, the removal of the wicked results in God's judgment. After the careful exegesis of this passage in Matthew 13:47-50, we come to the conclusion that through the parable of the dragnet, the Lord Jesus taught that when His angels come forth, they will remove the unbelievers from among the believers by taking them from the earth to their place of judgment, and the believers will be left on the earth to enter into Jesus' kingdom.

Line Of Evidence: Jesus' Teaching From **Matthew 24:37-41.**

In this passage, the Lord draws a comparison between the days of Noah and the Lord's coming with His angels. We read, **"For the coming of the Son of Man will be just like the days of Noah. For as in those days before the flood they were eating and drinking, marrying and giving in marriage, until the day that Noah entered the ark, and they did not understand until the flood came and took them all away; so will the coming of the Son of Man be. Then there will be two men in the field; one will be taken and one will be left. Two women will be grinding at the mill; one will be taken and one will be left."**

In this passage, our Lord tells us (two times, v37 and v39) that when He comes with His angels, it will be **"the same**

as the days of Noah!" This is significant because Jesus is drawing a comparison between the "days of Noah" and His coming!

Well, what does the Bible have to say to us about the days of Noah? If we can understand that, then we'll be able to understand what our Lord's coming is referring to! We know that despite Noah's warnings (2 Peter 2:5, Noah is called **"a preacher of righteousness"**) of God's coming judgment, the unbelievers devoted their attention to the normal affairs of life. They were oblivious as to what God was about to do. The problem was that the people of Noah's day lived without regard to God and Noah's warnings about the coming flood. In the same way, in spite of the tribulation period's warning signs of Jesus' coming with His angels for judgment (v32-35), many of the unbelievers of that period will devote their full attention to the normal affairs of life, oblivious as to what God is about to do. As a result, they will not prepare for the coming judgment by believing on the Lord. Next, just as the when the flood came and took away from the earth, all the unbelievers in judgment, likewise, at the Lord's coming with His angels all the unsaved will be removed from the earth in judgment!

Also, when the flood of Noah's day removed from the earth all the unsaved, only the saved (Noah and his family) were left on the earth to enter the next age of history. In like manner, when all the unsaved are removed from the earth in judgment connected with the Lord's coming with His angels, only the saved will be left on the earth to enter the Millennium, the next age of history!

In the context of Matthew 24:37-41, the Lord said that when He comes immediately after the tribulation, **"And He will send forth His angels with a great trumpet and they shall gather together His elect from the four winds, from one end of the sky to the other"** (Mt 24:31). Some have concluded that this passage refers to the gathering of church saints in the Rapture and that therefore, in light of this context, the taking of people from the field and mill is referring to church saints being taken from the earth in the Rapture. Upon careful exegesis, several lines of evidence will show that there's a sound reason for concluding that the gathering together of the elect in Matthew 24:31 is not in reference to the Rapture of church saints, but to the gathering of the believing remnant of Israel alive on the earth at the Lord's coming After the **Great Tribulation!**

First Line Of Evidence: We must understand that the word **"elect"** is not used only for the church saints in the Word of God. There are many passages which teach that the Lord God made the Jewish nation of Israel His elect people in contrast with every other nation. In Deuteronomy 7:6, we read, **"For you are a holy people to the Lord your God; the Lord your God has chosen you to be a people for His own possession out of all the peoples who are on the face of the earth."**

The concept of election speaks of being chosen by the Lord God to salvation. In light of this and other similar passages in Deuteronomy, G. Quell wrote that Deuteronomy **"established the concept of election in the sense of the designation of Israel as the people of God."** (Pg. 182). He further asserted that about election, **"the nations did not experience what Israel experienced."** (Pg. 182). See also 1 Chronicles 16:13, and Isaiah 45:4, where the Lord God called the nation **"Israel My chosen."**

The Hebrew word for "chosen" means, **"preferred or selected by God with an implication of rendering special favor." (Strong's Exhaustive Concordance Of the Bible; pg. 1479).** In Paul's letter to the church at Rome (Romans 11:28) the apostle referred to the nation of Israel as **"God's choice"** or His elect! Paul said, **"From the standpoint of the gospel they are enemies for your sake, but from the standpoint of God's choice they are beloved for the sake of the fathers" (Romans 11:28).** We see that from the perspective of God's eternal choice, the nation of Israel will always be His elect people. This is seen in the words of Paul in Romans 11:1 which says, **"I say then, God has not rejected His people, has He? May it never be! For I too am an Israelite, a descendent of Abraham, of the tribe of Benjamin."** Once again, we see that from the perspective of God's eternal choice, the Jewish people will always be His chosen or elect people!

Second Line Of Evidence:

In the passage of Matthew 24:31, the Lord spoke about His elect being gathered **"from the four winds, from one end of the sky to the other."** Arndt and Gingrich stated that in Matthew 24:31 this expression about the winds refers to **"the four directions or cardinal points." (Pg. 182).** In other words, the elect will be gathered from all over the world at Jesus' coming with His angels. In light of this statement, let's examine some Old Testament passages concerning Israel as God's elect.

First: Because of the nation of Israel's continual and determined rebellion towards the Lord, God said **"for I will execute judgments on you and scatter all your remnant to every wind" (Ezekiel 5:10).** Again in verse 12, God says "and one third I will scatter to every wind." Again, in Ezekiel 17:21, about Israel's rebellion, the Lord God says, "and the survivors will be scattered to every wind; and you will know that I the lord, have spoken." With respect to Israel, the prophet Zechariah said these words, "Ho there! Flee from the land of the north," declares the Lord, "for I have dispersed you as the four winds of the heavens, declares the Lord" (Zechariah 2:6).

Concerning the expression "the four winds" in the Old Testament, J. Barton Payne observed, "The four winds, describe the four quarters or four directions of the world (Jeremiah 49:36; Ezekiel 37:9), (Pg. 182)" In other words, in the Old Testament it had the same meaning as that found in Matthew 24:31. We know from history as well as the Bible that God indeed scattered the Jewish people all over the world. In Isaiah 43:5-7, God said that in the future, the nation of Israel would be gathered from the east, west, north, and south, from their worldwide scattering/dispersing. This is in reference to the faithful remnant of Israel. The passage says, "Do not fear, for I am with you; I will bring your offspring from the east, and gather you from the west. I will say to the north, "Give them up!" And to the south, 'Do not hold them back.' Bring My sons from afar and My daughters from the ends of the earth. Everyone who is called by My name, and whom I have created for My glory, whom I have formed, even whom I have made."

After further review of the passage in Matthew 24:31, we can conclude that the gathering of the Lord's elect is not referring to the rapture of church saints, but is about the believing remnant of Jews who'll be alive at the Lord's coming with His angels. When the rapture takes place, all church saints (Jews and Gentiles) will be taken from the earth! It will not, as Matthew 24:31 indicates, be limited just to the elect/saved of Israel! When the rapture happens, the church is removed from the earth.

An examination of Luke 17:26-37: This passage gives Luke's account to the same teaching of the Lord recorded in Matthew 24:37-41. We've already examined the Matthew 24:37-41 passage. We read, **"And just as it happened in the days of Noah, so it will be also in the days of the Son of Man: they were eating, they were drinking, they were marrying, they were being given in marriage, until the day that Noah entered the ark, and the flood destroyed them all. It was the same as happened in the days of Lot: they were eating, they were drinking, they were buying, they were selling, they were planting, they were building; but on the day that Lot went out from Sodom it rained fire and brimstone from heaven and destroyed them all. It will be just the same on the day that the Son of Man is revealed. On that day, the one who is on the housetop and whose goods are in the house must not go down to take them out; and likewise the one who is in the field must not turn back. Remember Lot's wife. Whoever seeks to keep his life will lose it, and whoever loses his life will preserve it. I tell you, on that night there will be two in one bed; one will be taken and the other will be left. There will be two women grinding at the same place; one will be taken and the other will be left. Two men will be in the field; one will be taken and the other will be left. And answering they said to Him, "Where Lord?" And He said to them, "Where the body is, there also the vultures will be gathered."'**

We see that in Luke, the Lord indicates that the same way God's judgment came upon the unsaved of Noah's day when Noah entered the ark, and just as it came upon the unsaved of Lot's time on the day Lot left out of Sodom, so God's judgment will come upon the unsaved on the earth

"on the day that the Son of Man is revealed" (v 30). We must take note of the fact that the passage mentions nothing about God's judgment coming upon the unsaved on the day the church is removed. Also, Noah and Lot were not raptured from the earth when God's judgment fell upon the unsaved. Instead, they remained on the earth while the unsaved were taken away through judgment. They continued on the earth into the next period of history!

In verse 37, Luke says something that Matthew omitted. After the Lord told them of the people being taken and left, the disciples asked, **"Where Lord?"** They wanted to know where those who are to be removed will be taken when the Lord comes. The Lord answered, **"Where the body is, there also the vultures will be gathered."** Vultures are birds which eat dead, rotting flesh. The term **"will be gathered"** points to the gathering of birds around a dead carcass. In other words, the Lord's answer shows that those people who are removed from the earth, (the bed, place of grinding, and the field) when He comes will be taken into the realm of death. God's judgment upon them will be death and their dead bodies will be eaten by vultures (Revelation 19:17-18, 21). These simply cannot be church saints who are taken away in the rapture!! This is because when the rapture happens, the bodies of church saints are not eaten by vultures but the bodies of dead church saints will be raised as immortal, incorruptible! The bodies of church saints who have not died before the rapture will be changed instantly into immortal, incorruptible bodies!

See 1 Thessalonians 4:14-16; 1 Corinthians 15:42-44, 51-53. So, those mentioned in Luke 17, as being taken away from the earth when the Lord comes, will be the unsaved, taken away in judgment. Those left on the earth will be the saved! ·They'll continue in the 1000 year reign of Christ.

We have examined passages that pertain to the rapture of the church John 14:1-4; 1 Corinthians 15:51-53; and 1 Thessalonians 4:13-18). We have examined passages that pertain to the Second Coming of Jesus with His holy angels (Matthew 13:24-30, 47-50; Matthew 24:37-41; Luke 1 7:26-3 7; and Revelation 19: 11 -21). When these two events are compared, they describe two very different scenarios. Because the Pretribulation Rapture view teaches that the church will be raptured from the earth before the seven-year 70th week of the Daniel 9 prophecy starts and that Jesus will come with His angels after the 70th week ends, it agrees with the following conclusions stated earlier: The rapture of the church and the second coming of Jesus with His angels must be two distinct events, and they must take place at two distinct times!

1. Jesus' coming at the rapture is to take saints from the earth to the Father's house in heaven, in contrast to the second coming, when the saints will come from heaven with Jesus to the earth.

2. At the rapture, those who are "in Christ," the church, will be resurrected from the dead, and living Christ followers will be given glorified bodies, in contrast to the second coming, when none will be given glorified bodies. The tribulation saints will enter the 1000-year kingdom with their natural bodies.

3. At the rapture, the world is left unjudged and living in sin, in contrast to the second coming, when the world is judged and righteousness is established.

4. At the rapture, only the church is caught up to heaven, in contrast to the second coming, when Old Testament saints and tribulation saints will be resurrected, but remain on the earth.

5. The rapture is shown in Scripture to be an imminent event, that is, there are no predicted events that precede the rapture, in contrast to the second coming before which many world-shaking prophetic events must be fulfilled as seen in Revelation chapter 6 through Revelation chapter 18.

6. The rapture is a New Testament truth, in contrast to the doctrine of second coming; which is revealed in both Testaments.

7. Before and after the rapture, Satan will continue to be active, but after the rapture, Satan will be allowed even greater activity, in contrast to the second coming, where Satan will be bound for 1000 years.

8. The purpose of the rapture is to take saints from the earth to heaven, in contrast to the second coming, which involves resurrection of the Old Testament saints and the tribulation saints who remain on the earth. Later, at the second coming, those who were raptured will join those still living in the world that will enter the 1000-year kingdom.

9. If all the saints had been raptured at the same time of the second coming and met Jesus in the air, the judgment of the Gentiles in Matthew 25:31-46 would be unnecessary, because there would have already been a separation of the saints from those not saved while Jesus was coming from heaven to earth (1 Thessalonians 4:16-17). The fact that this judgment takes place after the second coming, is proof that the rapture did not happen as part of the second coming, as Posttribulationlism teaches.

1 0. The rapture relates to the church, both living and dead, in contrast to the second coming, which relates primarily to Israel and the Gentiles.

11. The rapture is a blessed hope, a happy expectation, which could happen at any time, in contrast to the second coming, which can be realized only after the great tribulation when the majority of earth's population will have perished in one disaster or another.

We have seen that the passage in Matthew 24:37-42 does not teach about the rapture. We've seen that the historical illustration of Noah teaches that Noah and his family were left alive while the entire world was taken away in death and judgment! I This is exactly the order of events to be expected at the Lord's second coming as taught in the passage of Matthew 13:24-43 (parable of the wheat and tares), and the passage of Matthew 13:47-50 (parable of the dragnet), Luke's account of the same teaching of the Lord recorded in Matthew 24:37-41, (Luke 17:26-37). In all of these passages, at the final event in Jesus' second coming, unbelievers are taken away in judgment and the righteous believers remain. These passages consistently teach the same order of events for the coming of the Lord with His angels immediately after the great tribulation. All the living unsaved will be taken from the earth in judgment, and all the living saved will be left on the earth to enter the next period of history. In stark contrast, at the rapture of the church all the saved will be taken from the earth to meet Jesus in the air, and all the unsaved will be left on the earth to enter the next period of history. The order of things at the rapture of the church will be the reverse of the order of things at the Lord's coming immediately after the great tribulation. It is the combined force of all these lines of evidence which brings the conclusion that these passages are not in reference to the rapture of the church, but points toward the second coming of Jesus in judgment with His holy angels! It's the combined force of all these lines of evidence which leads to the conclusion that the rapture of the church and the coming of Jesus with His angels must be two distinct and separate events, and therefore must take place at two different times!

Chapter Three: What is the Tribulation?

For us to understand the time of rapture of the church, we must first understand what the Bible teaches about the tribulation. The word "tribulation" comes from the Greek word meaning "affliction, distress, or trouble." It's used in general for any type of testing, distress or affliction which people go through in life, and especially of the church and her problems with this fallen world system (John 16:33; Romans 5:3; Revelation 1:9, 2:9-10). However, the Bible also uses the term "the tribulation" to refer to **"a specific time of trouble, a special time of judgment from God"** that will visit the world, will be unprecedented in its trouble and will be culminated by the personal return of Christ Jesus to earth.

The Source of the Tribulation

The Word of God reveals the tribulation is a manifestation of the settled but determined wrath of God **using Satan and mankind as instruments of divine judgment.** This is shown in the situation where God used the Assyrians as the rod of His wrath (Isaiah 10:5-6). Isaiah informs us that God used Assyria as His instrument of judgment against Judah and Israel. Isaiah says **"Woe to Assyria, the rod of My anger and the staff in whose hands is My indignation, I send it against a godless nation and commission it against the people of My fury to capture booty and to seize plunder, and to trample them down like mud in the streets" (Isaiah 10:5-6).** The term **"godless nation"** is about Israel and Judah. God later did the same with the Babylonians against Judah (Habakkuk 1:6-11). The events of the tribulation (Revelation 6-19) are clearly specified as the sovereign actions of the Lamb of God who breaks the seals of the scroll which brings forth the judgments of God (Revelation 5:1-9; 6:1,3,5,7,9,12; 8:1).

The Character and Nature of the Tribulation

    A. **A time of unprecedented trouble** (Joel 2:1-2; Matthew 24:21; Zephaniah 1:14-15). Everything about the tribulation will be unprecedented! It'll be unprecedented in scope, intensity and magnitude!

    B. **A time of God's determined but settled wrath and the vindication of God's holiness** (Revelation 6:17; 1 Thessalonians 1:10; Revelation 14:7, 10; 19:2). God's wrath is against the sin and rebellion of mankind.

    C. **A time of extreme deception and delusion** (2 Thessalonians 2:9-12; Revelation 13:2-3. 11-18). This deception and delusion results from several things:

        a. The rapture or removal of the Holy Spirit indwelt church with its restraining influence (2 Thessalonians 2:6-8).

        b. The increase of demonic activity (2 Thessalonians 2:8-10).

        c. The blinding judgment of God (2 Thessalonians 2:11-12).

    D. **A time of extreme lawlessness and sin** (Revelation 9:20-21, 13:11-14; 2 Thessalonians 2:12; Matthew 24:12).

E. **A time of preparation for Israel's restoration and conversion** (Daniel 9:24-27; Deuteronomy 4:29-30; Jeremiah 30:3-11).

F. **A time of God's amazing grace and mercy** (Revelation 7:9-17; Matthew 24:14).

G. **A time of catastrophic destruction, desolation, darkness and terror** (Zephaniah 1:14-15; Joel 1:15).

Names used for the Tribulation

1. Daniel's 70th week (Daniel 9:24-27)
2. Jacob's distress (Jeremiah 30:7)
3. The hour of testing (Revelation 3:10)
4. Tribulation and Great tribulation (Matthew 24:9, 21, 29; Mark 13:19, 24; Revelation 7:14).
5. The Day of the Lord (Joel 1:15, 2:1; Zephaniah 1:14-15' 1 Thessalonians 5:2-3).

Key Participants and Personages of the Tribulation

A. **Unbelievers:** The tribulation will begin with only unbelievers since the church will have been taken away through the rapture and kept from this "hour of trial" (Revelation 3:10; 1 Thessalonians 1:10, 5:9; Romans 5:9; Ephesians 5:6; Colossians 3:4). Again, and again, the Bible states the church is not to endure God's wrath. For the Christ follower, there's no judgment unto wrath (Romans 8:1). We're not appointed to the time of God's wrath (1 Thessalonians 5:2, 9). When God's purpose for the church is completed, it'll be taken as a completed body to the Father's house at the rapture (John 14:2-

3; 1 Thessalonians 4:13-18). The rapture of the church clears the way for a restoration and resumption of the sovereign Lord's purpose for His elect nation, Israel.

B. Jews and Gentiles: The participants of the tribulation are further categorized by their racial heritage as either Jews or Gentiles. The Bible groups mankind into three categories: a) The church; b) Israel; c) Gentiles or "the nations" (1 Corinthians 10:32). In the tribulation, the church will be gone so the world will consist of only Jews (Israel) and Gentiles (the nations). An examination of Ephesians 2:11-22 reveals why the church is considered a new entity of people, a new man; a new creation where Jews and Gentiles are made one in Christ Jesus.

C. 144,000 bond servants of the Lord: 12,000 Jews from each of the 12 tribes of Israel gives us 144,000 Jews. These Jews are saved after the tribulation begins. They're sealed, which points to their salvation, identification, and divine protection for service during the rest of the tribulation. The context of Revelation chapter seven shows that God will use these bond servants to lead multitudes to Jesus from every nation, and tribes and peoples and tongues (Revelation 7:1-14). The verb **"to seal"** means to make an imprint in wax and was often done with a signet ring (a seal ring). It signified several ideas:

    a. **A completed transaction.** For the 144,000, it signified their salvation (Ephesians 4:30).

       b. **A mark of identification and ownership.** The 144,000 became the servants of God and God's people.

       c. **A mark of security and protection.** The sealing guaranteed their physical and spiritual protection. This is seen by the fact that God's judgment is restrained until the sealing has taken place (Revelation 7:3).

D. **The two witnesses**: The identity of these men has not been revealed to us. They are two men who will come onto the scene performing miracles like those of Moses and Elijah. Like Moses, they strike the earth with plagues, and like Elijah, they have the power to shut up the windows of heaven, preventing rain (Exodus 7; James 5:17-18; Revelation 11:1-14). They will prophesy during one half of the tribulation (3.5 years).

E. **Satan and his demons:** Obviously, as a time of great darkness and deception, Satan and his demons are key participants in this drama. All the lawlessness of this period results from Satanic involvement combined with the sinfulness of men (2 Thessalonians 2:9-12; Revelation 9:1-11, 12:3-17, 16:13-14, 13:1-2).

F. **The Beast:** This title refers to both a man and his evil system of operation that's opposed to God and His people. This evil satanic system of government is controlled by a Satan possessed man from whom the system derives its monstrous and vicious nature. He's also known as the Antichrist, the lawless one, and **"the one whose coming is in accord with the**

activity of Satan, with all power and signs and false wonders, and with all the deception of wickedness for those who perish, because they did not receive the love of the truth so as to be saved" (2 Thessalonians 2:9-10; Revelation 13:1-10; Daniel 2:40-43, 9:27).

G. **The false prophet:** This is a religious figure who vigorously promotes the person and ministry of the beast (Revelation 13:11-18). He will be Satan's mouthpiece and thus his message and words are false! Satan is the originator of all false religion (2 Corinthians 11:13-15). Jesus said of the devil, he **"does not stand in the truth because there is no truth in him. Whenever he speaks a lie, he speaks from his own nature, for he is liar and the father of lies" (John 8:44).** He is a wolf in sheep's clothing! Our Lord said, **"Beware of the false prophets, who come to you in sheep's clothing, but inwardly are ravenous wolves" (Matthew 7:15).**

H. **Fallen angels and Michael and his angels:** The Revelation of Jesus Christ (the book) is filled with the services of angels of God in service to God as well as the fallen angels who does service to Satan (Revelation 12:7-10).

I. **The Lord Jesus Christ:** He's the central figure of the revelation who's revealed in all His glory and majesty! He alone is worthy to open the seven-sealed scroll that begins the tribulation and He's the one who brings it to an end and establishes the

Kingdom of God on earth! He's the King of kings, and the Lion who is also a Lamb (Revelation 5:1-14)!

The Time of The Tribulation

The tribulation takes place after the catching away of, or the removal of the church (1 Thessalonians 4:13-18; 5:1-9). It's followed by the 1000-year reign of the Lord Jesus Christ (Revelation 20:1-4; Ezekiel 20:33-38). In order to fully understand this, we must know that Israel and the church are two separate and distinct groups of peoples (1 Corinthians 10:32; Romans 9; 10; 11). The tribulation does not deal with the church at all, but with the purging and restoration of God's remnant people Israel! The Lord's purposes for the tribulation do not involve the church. The tribulation is for Israel's redemption. Jeremiah 30:7-9 says, **"Alas! For that day is great, there is none like it; And it is the time of Jacob's distress, but he will be saved from it. It shall come about on that day, declares the Lord of Hosts, that I will break his yoke from off their neck and will tear off their bonds; and strangers will no longer make them their slaves. But they shall serve the Lord their God and David their king, whom I will raise up for them."** First, let's take notice of the fact that this period (the tribulation) is described as **"the time of Jacob's distress."** The name **"Jacob"** is symbolic of the nation of Israel. This period of **unprecedented distress** for the nation of Israel is set in a context of Israel's final redemption and restoration. We know this time to be that of the tribulation! Further proof can be found in the words, **"David their king."** This phrase is about Jesus, the Messiah, the greater David in David's dynasty ultimately fulfills this prophecy (2 Samuel 7:12, 13, 16). While the church does experience tribulation **in general** during this present fallen world system (John 16:33; Romans 5:3; Revelation 1:9; 2:9-10), she is never mentioned as taking part in Jacob's distress, which includes the Great Tribulation, the Day of the Lord, Daniel's 70th week, and the hour of testing which is about to come upon the whole world! The church does not fit into this scenario, and is left out of God's purposes for the tribulation. Because of this reason, the church would need to be taken away, caught up, and raptured before the tribulation begins!

A Further Look at The Distinctions Between Israel And the Church

1. Israel is a nation, but the church is not.
2. The national language of Israel is Hebrew, but the church does not have a common language.
3. Israel has a political government, but the church does not.
4. God established and regulated the political government of Israel, but the Lord God has not done this for the church.
5. Israel has a common background, but the church does not. The church is made of people from many different ethnic groups, traditions and backgrounds.
6. Israel has a military system to engage in warfare against other nations, but the church does not.
7. Israel did not embrace their Messiah, but the church received Christ.
8. Israel was the first to show hostility to the church, which also shows distinction.

9. The Bible categorizes mankind today in three categories: a) The church; b) Israel; c) Gentiles (1 Corinthians 10:32). Further distinctiveness!

What are the implications of these biblical lines of distinction? Simply that God's program and plans for Israel are different than His program and plans for the church. If we do not see that the two are separate and distinct, that God has two different programs to work out, then the timing of when the church is removed from the earth (caught up) will remain a mystery to us! We'll continue looking for events that pertain to Israel and not the church! This is not the wisdom of God for us. Only the pretribulation rapture accounts for the distinctions that exist between Israel and the church! The pretribulation rapture of the church is the only view of the rapture that has the church being taken away from the earth before the 70th week of Daniel's prophecy begins, before God resumes His 70-week program with Daniel's people (Israel). In other words, the pretribulation view of the catching away of the church is the only view that keeps God's specific 70-week program for Israel separate and distinct from His program for the church. All other rapture views have the church going through at least a portion of the 70th week if not all of the 70th week! This is an error for it mixes God's 70-week program for Israel together with His program and plan for the church! What is the point of putting the church into the time of Jacob's distress? Why is it called the time of **Jacob's distress?**

Whenever the purpose for something is ignored or not known, abnormal use will always be the result. The same applies to knowing that God's purpose for the tribulation does not include the church. A familiar thought held by many Christ followers is as follows: "The church will go through the tribulation because the Bible says that the

church will be persecuted and suffer for following Jesus."
The problem with thinking this way is that while it may
seem to have the veneer of biblical truth, at the core it
indicates a lack of understanding of God's purpose for the
tribulation. Will Christ followers suffer tribulation for
following Christ? Yes, indeed! Will Christ followers
experience the special time of tribulation that deals with
God's judgment that will visit the entire world? No!

The tribulation in Bible prophecy is the period of time that
begins after the church is removed from the earth by the
Lord Jesus and taken to His Father's house. The tribulation
in Bible prophecy will end seven years later at the second
coming of Jesus Christ to end it. The second coming of the
Lord Jesus Christ is examined in more detail in another
chapter. The most extensive commentary on the tribulation
is found in the writings of apostle John, specifically in the
book of Revelation chapters 6-19. In these awesome
chapters, John gives a very detailed exposition of the
tribulation. Daniel's "70 week" prophecy in Daniel 9:24-
27 gives us the framework within the tribulation that takes
place. In other words, to gain a better understanding of
what apostle John delivers in Revelation chapters 6-9, we
need a thorough understanding of the prophecy of Daniel
9:24-27.

A Critical Exegesis of the 70 Weeks Prophecy of Daniel Chapter Nine

Towards the end of Israel's captivity in Babylon, in
response to Daniel's concern about Israel's future, God sent
Daniel a prophecy through the angel Gabriel (Daniel 9:20-
21). This prophecy is recorded for us in Daniel 9:24-27.
Let's examine some significant facts about this prophecy.

It reads, **"Seventy weeks have been decreed for your people and your holy city, to finish the transgression, to make an end of sin, to make atonement for iniquity, to bring in everlasting righteousness, to seal up the vision and prophecy and to anoint the most holy place." "So you are to know and discern that from the issuing of a decree to restore and rebuild Jerusalem until Messiah the Prince there will be seven weeks and sixty-two weeks; it will be built again, with plaza and moat, even in times of distress." Then after the sixty-two weeks the Messiah will be cut off and have nothing, and the people of the prince who is to come will destroy the city and the sanctuary. And its end will come with a flood; even to the end there will be war; desolations are determined."**

"And he will make a firm covenant with the many for one week, but in the middle of the week he will put a stop to sacrifice and grain offering; and on the wing of abominations will come one who makes desolate, even until a complete destruction, one that is decreed, is poured out on the one who makes desolate" (Daniel 9:24-27).

Fact Number One: This prophecy involved **"seventy weeks"** (literally "seventy sevens") of time (verse 24). Seventy sevens are equivalent to seventy times seven or 490. The prophecy consisted of 490 units of time. The question becomes, "How much time is involved in these 490 units?" That's a very good question. Now, let's find the answer. Seventy sevens of **years** would've been meaningful to God's people, Israel. This is confirmed by the fact that there were seventy **years** of captivity discussed earlier in the chapter (Daniel 9:2) Daniel's study focused on the years prophesied for the captivity by Jeremiah in Jeremiah 25:11-12; 29:10. The seventy sevens is equivalent to seventy times seven years or 490 years, with the beginning of the time of the **"decree to restore and rebuild Jerusalem"** found in verse 25 and culmination of 490 years later in verse 27. The fact that Daniel had been thinking in terms of years in the context of this seventy-week prophecy (Daniel 9:1-2), gives the conclusion that the units of time involved is 490 years.

Fact Number Two: According to the words spoken in verse 24, the 70 weeks (490 years) were decreed for Daniel's people and the holy city. There is no mention of any of the 490 years being for the church! The 490 years were determined for Israel, not the church. Who were Daniel's people? What is the holy city? Daniel's people are none other than Israel and the holy city is none other than Jerusalem. Why is this information important to know? Recall that we showed many points of evidence that the church and Israel are distinct. We see from the prophecy of Daniel 9:24-27, the Lord did not choose any of the 490 years to involve the church! Daniel's people and the holy city are distinct from the church! It's important that we understand this distinction considering this prophecy. The tribulation is God's program and purpose for Israel. This prophecy is about the future of Israel in the end of the age. The six things mentioned in verse 24 have to do with Israel's restoration and conversion to Christ Jesus. Let's examine them.

1. **"Finish the transgression."** The Bible declares in many places, the long trends of disobedience and rebellion of Israel toward God. God is going to end it. This will happen during the tribulation.
2. **"Make an end of sin."** God will finally judge their sin against Him.

3. **"Make atonement for iniquity."** This covering of sin will be realized when the remnant of Israel receives Jesus as Lord and Savior.

4. **"Bring in righteousness."** The righteousness of God which comes from salvation in Christ as the remnant looks to Jesus as Lord.

5. **"Seal up the vision."** God will bring these things to completion for the remnant of Israel. No more revelation is needed.

6. **"Anoint the most holy place."** This is the place which functions as the center of worship in the Lord's millennial kingdom on earth. These six things speak of the resumption and completion of God's program for Israel.

Fact Number Three: In Daniel 9:25, Gabriel told Daniel that the time from the start of the 70 weeks of years until **"Messiah the prince"** would be **"seven weeks and sixty-two weeks."** What does this period equal? Seven weeks plus sixty-two weeks equals sixty-nine weeks! We have 69 weeks of years or 483 years. In other words, 483 years after the start of the 490 years (70 weeks), Messiah the Prince would be present in the world. Who is **Messiah the Prince**? He's none other than Jesus Christ. Zechariah 9:9 is about Jesus' first coming to His people Israel. It says, **"Rejoice greatly, O daughter of Zion! Shout in triumph, O daughter of Jerusalem! Behold, your king is coming to you; He is just and endowed with salvation, humble and mounted on a donkey, even on a colt, the foal of a donkey."**

Was Messiah ever known to Israel as its prince or king? Yes, He was! The Hebrew word translated **"Prince"** in Daniel 9:25 means "leader, ruler." The Hebrew word translated **"king"** in Zechariah 9:9 means "royal ruler, leader." The fulfillment of the prophecy in Zechariah 9:9 is found in Matthew 21:5-9. Messiah the Prince fulfilled this part of the 70 weeks prophecy (483 years) of Daniel 9:25. Verse 25 also mentions, **"from the issuing of a decree to restore and rebuild Jerusalem until Messiah the Prince."** This accounts for the seven weeks of years or 49 years from the issuing of the decree to rebuild Jerusalem (Nehemiah 2:1-8). Adding the 49 years (seven weeks of years) to the 434 years (sixty-two weeks of years) gives us a total of 483 years (sixty-nine weeks of years). This time has already been accounted for!

Fact Number Four: Daniel 9:26 says, **"Then after the sixty-two weeks the Messiah will be cut off."** Messiah will be cut off after the end of the 483 years (69 weeks of years). What does the term **"cut off"** mean? It is a term used in the Bible for the death penalty (Leviticus 7:20-21; 25, 27). It often portrayed a violent death (1 Samuel 17:51; Nahum 3:15). In Daniel's 70 weeks prophecy, it clearly refers to Messiah's brutal execution. We know that Messiah was falsely accused and condemned to the death penalty. That happened over 2000 years ago. **When Messiah was crucified, He was cut off and that accounted for the first 483 years (sixty-nine of the seventy weeks of years prophesied by Daniel). Recall, that God determined the entire 490 years (seventy weeks of years) for Israel. That leaves us with 7 years (one week) left unfulfilled. That last week (7 years) has not yet come to pass. But it will come to pass because**

that last week is the tribulation period! This last week has to do with the arrival of another prince. Who is this prince? He's the white horse rider of Revelation 6:2. Do we have any evidence for this gap of time that's between the 69th and 70th week? This gap of time has now reached at least 2000 years. **It's not unusual for Bible prophesies to contain gaps of time between fulfillments.**

Let's examine Isaiah 9:6. It reads **"For a child will be born to us."** This phrase is about the Lord Jesus' **first coming.** But verse 6 continues with these words, **"...and the government will rest on His shoulders."** This second phrase is about the Lord Jesus' **second coming** to rule and reign. This passage of Scripture demonstrates that Bible prophecies can contain gaps in time between their fulfillments. See Zechariah 9:9-10 for a similar example of a prophecy that contains a gap in time between its fulfillments! The same is found in the 70 weeks prophecy of Daniel 9:24-27. The last week (7 years) has not taken place and is still in the future. **The last week is part of the future of humanity!** It is also identified as the tribulation! Recall, that the tribulation period is 7 years in length of time...the 70th week of Daniel's prophecy. The rapture of the church is what brings God's program for the church to a close. After the rapture of the church, God will again direct His attention to Israel in preparation for a time of purging to save His remnant. While the 7-year tribulation is taking place, the Word of God shows the church is occupied in heaven at the Father's house. The church is shown in heaven worshipping the Lamb and the one who sits on the throne! There's the Bema judgment (2 Corinthians 5:10), the marriage of Jesus' bride, the church (Revelation 19:7-9), and there's the following of the Lord Jesus Christ into the Battle which takes place at Armageddon at the end of the tribulation (Revelation 19:11-21). The church and angelic forces follow the Lord Jesus Christ into His second coming to earth (Revelation 19:14).

Jesus Christ as the Kinsman-Redeemer and last Adam (Understanding God's program of land redemption for Israel and His program of redemption for the world).

A look at the primary responsibilities of the Kinsman-Redeemer: First, there was a redemption price needed for the land which gives the right of tenant possession. Next, gaining the right of tenant possession, the Kinsman-redeemer had to take possession of the land and exercise authority over it. This leads us to the identification of the seven-sealed scroll of Revelation 5. There is a parallel between the Lord's program of land redemption for the Jewish people and His program of redemption for the entire world.

We've already mentioned the fact that there was a redemption price needed to redeem the land. In the same way that the Jewish kinsman-redeemer was required to pay a redemption price to buy back the lost inheritance of his kin, so the Lord Jesus, as the Kinsman-Redeemer of humanity and their tenant possession of earth, had to pay a redemption price needed to buy back the lost (forfeited) inheritance of humanity. Christ paid the redemption price by the shedding of His precious blood (Ephesians 1:7; Colossians 1:14; Revelation 5:9). The apostle Peter describes it with these words **"Knowing that you were not redeemed with perishable things like silver or gold from your futile way of life inherited from your forefathers, but with the precious blood, as of a lamb unblemished and spotless, the blood of Christ" (1 Peter 1:18-19).**

Through His precious blood, Christ paid the redemption price to buy back tenant possession of the earth which Adam lost. Jeremiah's scrolls were the evidence that he paid the redemption price and because he did, that gave him the authority of possession of the land (Jeremiah 32:1-15). In the same way, the scroll that only Christ could take and break its seals is the evidence that He paid the redemption price and because He did, that gives Him and only Him the right of tenant possession of earth. That's what the scroll of Revelation 5 represents! It's no wonder all of heaven breaks loose in worship of the Lamb of God who was found worthy to take the scroll and to break its seals (Revelation 5:9)!

Revelation 5:1-14

Revelation chapters 6-19 unfold the threatening and devastating events of the seven-year tribulation period. The tribulation period describes God's wrath and judgment on an unbelieving world. However, before these tribulation events take place, we're given God's perspective which shows the justice of these events and their necessity. Revelation chapters 4 and 5 set the stage for what's about to take place in chapters 6-22. In chapter 4 our attention is focused on the throne in heaven and its Occupant. Revelation 4:8 emphasizes the holiness of God. Revelation 4:9-10 emphasizes, **"Him who lives forever and ever"** and points to the fact that God is eternal and existed before creation. God is contrasted with creation, which has a beginning. Revelation 4:11 emphasizes the Creator God who **"created all things"** and that He created all things for His own benefit. God is the only Being with the wisdom, power and sovereignty to create all things for His purpose. God's sovereignty to govern all of creation is shown in both chapters 4 and 5. The word **"throne"** is used 13 times in chapter four and 4 times in chapter five! The word "throne" means dominion, sovereignty, and rule. Also, the two doxologies in Revelation 4:11 and 5:13 contain words that ascribe sovereign power and authority to God. We see the superior power of God to which the final victory belongs. In 4:11 we read these words, **"Worthy are You, our Lord and our God, to receive glory and honor and power."** In 5:13 we read these words, **"To Him who sits on the throne, and the Lamb, be blessing and honor and glory and dominion forever and ever."** These words describe the awesome power God uses to govern His creation. The right to rule over all that is belongs to God! As Creator and Sovereign, God has the right to exercise His power to crush any opposition, and any rebellion to His rule. Chapters 4 and 5 are the prelude to God's use of power in defeating any opposition to His rule over the earth and the establishment of His King to rule the earth! Praise God forevermore!

The Seven Sealed Scroll (Revelation 5:1)

"I saw in the right hand of Him who sat on the throne a book written inside and on the back, sealed up with seven seals." The seven-sealed scroll that's held in the right hand of Him who sat on the throne, catches John's attention. The One sitting on the throne is the Almighty Sovereign God of all creation. What's the significance of this scene? The significance is found in what God is holding in His hand. The significance is found in the **"book written inside and on the back, sealed up with seven seals."** The term **"right hand"** is symbolic of the power and justice of God. The seven-sealed book (literally, a scroll, the Greek biblion) contains the prophecy of events to be unfolded in chapters 6-22 of the Revelation. This scroll contains the plans and purposes of God for crushing the enemies of Christ and establishing His Kingdom on the earth (Revelation 20:1-10). This scroll is what Christ opens in Revelation chapter 6, resulting in the terrible and devastating judgments from God that will come upon the earth (the tribulation). In other words, the scroll undoubtedly contains prophecies of the judgments of the tribulation needed to bring rebellious mankind to his knees, destroy Satan's kingdom and to establish God's King on the throne. The period of God's long-suffering has come to an end.

"...a book written inside and on the back," John was impressed that this scroll contained writing on both sides. What does this teach us? Writing on both sides signifies the fullness of the judgments as well as their ability to accomplish the purposes of God (Ezekiel 2:9-10). **"...sealed up with seven seals..."** The number seven symbolizes completeness or perfection. This is seen throughout the Bible. The hidden things of God are securely kept until God Himself discloses them. Let's examine another reason for the seven seals. It has to do with the Roman cultural practices during John's time on earth. The Roman custom of making wills included a ceremony that consisted of seven witnesses and a testator. There was a corresponding seal for each of the seven witnesses. The Jewish custom of making wills was somewhat different. If a Jewish family was ever to lose its possessions or property by some misfortune, their possessions or property could only be taken on a non-permanent basis. The Old Testament law of jubilee and the kinsman redeemer was a protection against permanently losing one's property or possessions (Leviticus 25). However, their losses were listed in a scroll and sealed seven times. The conditions needed to buy back (redeem) the land and their possessions were written on the outside of the scroll. When a qualified redeemer could be located, one who could meet the requirements of redemption, the one who had taken the possessions was required to return it to the original owner. This is the concept of the kinsman redeemer.

Examination of the principle and application of the Kinsman Redeemer

1. The earth and its rule was given to Adam and to his descendants (Genesis 1:26-30; Hebrews 2:7-8). In this we're shown the divine purpose for man decreed (Hebrews 2:6-8).
2. The earth as well as humanity was not designed to be governed by angelic beings, Satan and his fallen angels (Hebrews 2:5, 8, 14-15; Revelation 9:1-11; 12:1-10). In this we're shown the divine purpose delayed. "But now we do not yet see all things subjected to Him" (Hebrews 1:8).
3. Within humanity, someone must be found, a kinsman redeemer; a person who's qualified to buy back (redeem) the lost inheritance (earth and its rule), someone who was true humanity, and at the same time, free to redeem; not a sinful man, or an angelic being (Hebrews 2:9, 14-17).

Notice the qualifications listed in Revelation 5:9-10, **"Worthy are You to take the book and to break its seals; for You were slain, and purchased for God with Your blood men from every tribe and tongue and people and nation. You have made them to be a kingdom of priests to our God; and they will reign upon the earth."** Who is this person that the four living creatures and the 24 elders are singing about? He's none other than Christ Jesus, our Kinsman Redeemer! **In this**

we're shown the divine purpose for humanity accomplished (Hebrews 2:9, 14, 17), our redemption, our lost inheritance of (earth and its rule).

"And I saw a strong angel proclaiming with a loud voice, "Who is worthy to open the book and break its seals? And no one in heaven or on the earth or under the earth was able to open the book or to look into it" (Revelation 5:2-3).

The word **"able"** means the ability to perform or do something whether by power, strength, ability or by authority or permission. These are the conditions that must be met! Search was made in every conceivable place in the universe, but none was found qualified or capable. A person with sufficient authority and worthiness was needed! A person was needed to open the book by breaking its seals to unleash the devastating tribulation judgments of God. **God could've used any prophet to reveal the contents of the book, but a person was needed who had the power and authority to not only reveal these judgments, but to bring them to pass.** Think about what's going on in this scene! If no one is found worthy to open the book and break its seals, then God's plan for the future of humanity would not happen! God's plan for the millennial kingdom does not take place! God's plan for the uprooting and removal of this present world system does not happen! God's plan of destroying Satan and the elimination of sin does not happen! God's promise to David that a King from his lineage will sit upon the throne in the millennial kingdom does not happen! With these things in mind, it's no wonder that John **"began to weep greatly."** If I was John, I would have wept greatly also! **"Then I began to weep greatly because no one was found worthy to open the book or to look into it" (Revelation 5:4).**

John's weeping indicates the effect on him, a godly man who's longing for the righteousness of God to be manifested in the world. John longs for justice to be manifested in the removal of ungodliness in the world. **John's weeping shows us what we all know, and that's the inability of anyone else in the entire universe to solve man's ultimate problem!** It was only when Adam lost dominion in the earth (through sin) that man began to experience pain, suffering, sorrow, tears, and death. Adam subjected humanity to the onslaught of the hard control and murderous intentions of the devil. Ever since, man has sought answers to his problems of being dominated by Satan and the sin nature. The problem is that these searches continue to be in all the wrong places. Man, has put his trust in man, in human governments and human viewpoint, in wealth, pleasure, and human philosophies, but the tears of man's suffering continue to flow. The wounds and scars of being dominated by the devil and the sin nature are evident! Just examine the landscape of humanity! The solution to humanity's dilemma is not to be found in man or the wisdom of man, but in the Lamb who is also the Lion, the Savior, Christ Jesus! Hallelujah!

"And one of the elders said to me, 'Stop weeping; behold, the Lion that is from the tribe of Judah, the root of David, has overcome so as to open the book and its seven seals.' And I saw between the throne (with the four living creatures) and the elders a Lamb standing, as if slain, having seven horns and seven eyes, which are the seven Spirits of God, sent out into all the earth. And He came and took the book out of the right hand of Him who sat on the throne" (Revelation 5:5-7).

Here, we're given the only solution to the problems that plague humanity. He's the Lion who is also a Lamb!

59

Apostle John is told to stop weeping because the one who turns tears of pain and sorrow into tears of joy is now on the scene! John is told to stop weeping because the one who turns our weeping into laughter is on the scene. The one of whom king David said, **"His favor is for a lifetime; Weeping may last for the night, But joy comes in the morning" (Psalm 30:5)** is on the scene! John gives contrasting pictures of Jesus. He calls Jesus **"the Lion."** This is about His second coming to rule and reign over the earth. As the Lion, Jesus is majesty, sovereign, and judge. John also calls Jesus **"a Lamb!"** This is about His first coming to take away the sins of the world (John 1:29). As the Lamb, Jesus is Savior. As the Lamb, Jesus was judged. As the Lamb, Jesus is God's perfect sacrifice to remove our sins! Praise God forevermore! The person of Jesus is on full display! He is **"the Lion from the tribe of Judah."** The lion is the king of beasts, and Judah is seen as the royal tribe.

In Genesis 49:9-10, we're given the prophecy that the future King of Israel and of the earth would come from the tribe of Judah. This prophecy is about Jesus Christ who was of David's lineage. Jesus was David's descendant in two ways. Jesus was David's legal descendant through being adopted by Joseph, and David's physical descendant through His mother Mary (Matthew 1; Luke 3:23). Next, Jesus is called **"the Root of David."** This is about the passage in Isaiah 11:1, where it's said that from Jesse, the father of David, the future King of the earth, would rise like a shoot from the root of a cut down tree. We know that the Davidic line would be cut down so that no man would occupy the throne of David (Jeremiah 22:24-30), however from David's roots would come Messiah. **He who came after David as his offspring was also before David as the Root!** Jesus said, **"I am the root and the descendant of David, the bright and morning star" (Revelation 22:16).**

How awesome is this? What else does John see? He sees **"A Lamb standing, as if slain."** What does this mean? The word **"standing"** means "to stand." The Lord had been slain, but is now seen standing and alive! Death tried but could not keep Jesus from rising from among the dead ones. Peter says, **"But God raised Him up again, putting an end to the agony of death, since it was impossible for Him to be held in its power" (Acts 2:24).**

The Lamb of God is seen standing as the resurrected and glorious Lord! John said **"He had seven horns."** What does this mean? Horns are symbolic of authority, power, rule and government. The word seven is symbolic of perfection or completion. What we're seeing is that the rule and government of Jesus is perfect. He's the perfect ruler (Isaiah 11:3-6; Revelation 19:15). This is what the world longs for, but continues looking in all the wrong places. John sees, **"And seven eyes."** Eyes are symbolic of the knowledge, wisdom, insight, and discernment of the Lord. The knowledge, wisdom, and insight of the Lord are perfect, as seen by the number seven. Paul tells us that **"in Him are hidden all the treasures of wisdom and knowledge" (Colossians 2:3).** John says, **"And He came and took the book out of the right hand of Him who sat on the throne."** Wow! Here we're seeing the transfer of authority from the Father to His son to not only reveal the future, but also to carry out the judgments of the tribulation. The devastating judgments of the tribulation will end with the establishment of the millennial kingdom and with Christ reigning on the throne of David in Jerusalem. Complete and total authority over the entire earth will be realized by Christ, the King.

"When He had taken the book, the four living creatures and the twenty-four elders fell down before the Lamb, each one holding a harp and golden bowls full of

incense, which are the prayers of the saints. And they sang a new song, saying, "Worthy are You to take the book and break its seals; for You were slain, and purchased for God with Your blood men from every tribe and tongue and people and nation. You have made them to be a kingdom and priests to our God; and they will reign upon the earth" (Revelation 5:8-10).

The Lamb of God is worthy of praise! He is worshipped by the four living creatures as well as the twenty-four elders. The twenty-four elders represent the raptured, glorified church. Notice what the church is holding. They're holding **"the prayers of the saints."** The context of this passage shows that these prayers symbolize all that the redeemed have prayed with respect to final redemption, prayers offered to the Lord for righteousness to reign on the earth. These are prayers for God to crush His enemies and to establish Christ as King over the entire earth. These prayers would be in line with the example prayer Jesus shared with the disciples (Matthew 6:10). Praise God forevermore.

The Lamb of God is worshipped for His finished work on the cross. The Lamb of God is worshipped for His worthiness to take the book and break its seals. The taking of the book and the breaking of its seals are in reference to the work that Christ is about to do as King of kings and Judge of all. Their worship of the Lamb is in response to His taking of the book from the right hand of God. The sacrificial death of Christ as a substitute for sinners made Him worthy to take the book and to loose the seals! Notice that John says **"You have made them to be a kingdom and priests to our God; and they will reign upon the earth."** As **"priest"** the believer in Christ has access to God and can represent Him here on the earth. During the millennial kingdom of Christ, Christ followers will reign with Him. The church is not ruling and reigning on the earth today. The teaching that the church is to be reigning on the earth today is false. God has not called the church to reign during this age. The church is called to represent Christ to the world.

"Then I looked and I heard the voice of many angels around the throne and the living creatures and the elders; and the number of them was myriads of myriads, and thousands of thousands, saying with a loud voice, "Worthy is the Lamb that was slain to receive power and riches and wisdom and might and honor and glory and blessing" (Revelation 5:11-12).

An innumerable company of angels now joins the living creatures and the twenty-four elders in praise, worship and adoration to the Lamb. The Greek term for **"myriad"** means 10,000. "Myriad of myriad" would equal 10,000 times 10,000. That equals 100 million. But John says **"myriads of myriads."** This equals hundreds of millions times hundreds of millions. This number is very easily in the billions! But John doesn't stop there! He says that there are still **"thousands of thousands."** In other words, this is a staggering number which goes beyond our ability to comprehend. What an awesome choir this is! Notice the word **"voice"** is singular. This means that they are speaking as one, in perfect unity! Imagine the intensity and degree of sound of this praise to the Lamb! I don't know about you but I can't wait to get there and worship with that group! Also, take notice of the words being used to exalt the Lamb. The Lamb is **"worthy to receive power."** He's worthy to receive **"wealth."** The wealth of the universe belongs to Him. The Lamb is worthy to receive **"wisdom."** He's worthy to receive **"strength and honor and glory and praise!"** The Lamb of God is worthy!

"And every created thing which is in heaven and on the earth and under the earth and on the sea, and all things in them, I heard saying, 'To Him who also sits on the throne, and to the Lamb, be blessing and honor and glory and dominion forever and ever. And the four living creatures kept saying, "Amen." And the elders fell down and worshipped" (Revelation 5:13-14).

We have more giving of praise to the One on the throne and to the Lamb! Wow!! All creation will worship the Father and the Son. The **"Amen"** signifies "truly, truly." This is the response of heaven asserting the validity of the worship! In conclusion: Donald Grey Barnhouse said: "Never will such music have been heard in the universe. Never will so many voices have intoned such mighty praise. The armies of armies come to the last note. The mightiest of God's creatures sound the amen. We gaze upon the scene with no voice for utterance and, prostrate, we worship the Lord Jesus Christ who now proceeds to the most awful scenes of Judgment with action that's rooted in His cross." (Revelation, An Expository Commentary, Zondervan, Grand Rapids, 1971, p. 113.) We have clearly seen from this chapter, that in heaven, the Father's house, all saints in their glorified state (no sin nature), will be busy and active with worshipping, praising, and giving glory to God. However, that's not something we should wait until that time to do. We should be living and doing all things to the glory of God (1 Corinthians 10:31).

An Examination of the Six Seals (Revelation 6:1-17)

The Start of the Tribulation

"Then I saw when the Lamb broke one of the seven seals, and I heard one of the four living creatures saying as with a loud voice of thunder, "Come." I looked, and

behold, a white horse, and he who sat on it had a bow; and a crown was given to him, and he went out conquering and to conquer" (Revelation 6:1-2).

This passage details the rise of the Antichrist and his false peace. This passage begins the devastating tribulation judgments. Before we continue, we must understand that these judgments are telescopic in nature. What this means is the 7th seal judgment incorporates all seven trumpet judgments and the 7th trumpet incorporates all seven bowl judgments. In other words, out of the 7th seal will come another series of seven trumpets and out of the 7th trumpet will come another series of seven bowls! Walvoord writes: "Actually, however, the seven seals comprehend the whole, as all the trumpets and all the vials (bowls) are comprehended in the seventh seal. The seven-sealed book (Revelation 5) therefore is the comprehensive program of God culminating in the second coming of Christ." (John F. Walvoord, The Revelation of Jesus Christ, Moody Press, Chicago, 1966, p. 124.)

This author agrees with Walvoord's statement. Let's continue the exegesis of Revelation 6:1-2. John wants us to **"behold"** or look at with amazement what he saw! He wants us to understand its importance. The seals portray to us the fact that God's future judgments were ordained in advance, but securely held back until God's time of releasing them. Now they are opened for us so that we can see by faith their devastating effects in advance! He says, **"...and behold, a white horse."** Throughout the Scriptures, **"white"** is symbolic of righteousness and peace. Because of this, many have wrongly identified this rider as Jesus Christ. **This rider is not Christ, but the Antichrist! He is the false Christ who arrives as a peacemaker, but**

in reality, is one who conquers! Let's examine some lines of evidence why this white horse rider is not Christ.

1. This happens too soon in the tribulation. During this period, Christ is in heaven breaking the seals of the scroll which causes the release of this white horse rider (Revelation 5:5, 9).

2. This rider, as well as the riders that follow, are instruments of evil and judgment. Christ is not an instrument of evil and judgment!

3. The white horse rider (Christ) in Revelation 19 comes to end the tribulation judgments. Here, the tribulation judgments are just beginning.

4. The crowns of the riders are different! The crown that this rider wears is a single victor's crown, as opposed to the many royal crowns of a sovereign which the rider of Revelation 19 wears. **The rider in our passage is the Antichrist.** In Daniel 9:26, this person is called the **"prince who is to come."** He's the one who **"will make a firm covenant with the many for one week"** (seven years), Daniel 9:27. The Daniel 9:24-27 prophecy was covered earlier, in more detail, under the section entitled **"A Critical Examination of the 70 weeks prophecy of Daniel chapter Nine."**

5. This white horse rider comes on the scene with a hidden agenda. His purpose is not to bring peace to the world, but rather world domination, as seen in the words **"conquering and to conquer."** This rider **"had a bow"** but no arrows are mentioned. How can this rider conquer without arrows? He does it through diplomacy and propaganda instead of open warfare. As we shall later see, open

warfare eventually comes. Today our world is ripe for the arrival of such a man claiming that his way of government will bring peace to the world. Everything in our world is suggesting the emergence of a one-world government, a one-world religion and a one-world ruler. It's on the way.

"When He broke the second seal, I heard the second living creature saying, "Come." And another, a red horse, went out; and to him who sat on it, it was granted to take peace from the earth, and that men would slay one another; and a great sword was given to him" (Revelation 6:3-4).

At this point, let me remind the reader that the sovereign Lamb is in control of these judgments as He is the one that breaks the seals. Notice the word **"Come."** It refers to each of the four horsemen. The four living creatures acting under the authority of the Lamb are successively calling these human instruments to move in their God appointed role. This stresses that they can't move until the sovereign God allows! As such, the command **"Come"** could be translated **"Go forth."** Notice the phrase **"it was granted to take peace."** This red horse rider operates under the sovereign control of the Lamb of God! In other words, if making war was not granted it would not happen! The phrase **"a red horse"** speaks of warfare as red is clearly symbolic of bloodshed. Jesus spoke of this period with these words, **"For nation will rise against nation, and kingdom against kingdom, and in various places there will be famines and earthquakes" (Matthew 24:7).**

Though wars have always played a part of our existence, warfare plays a huge part as history races toward eternity. Hal Lindsey reminds us, "The history of man ever since the

Fall has been a continuous horror of murder, war and the conquest of the weak by the strong. **War is the chief legacy of human history.** Its bloody trail is woven through the fabric of virtually every generation. Even man's greatest scientific achievements have been driven by the pursuit of more deadly weapons. This fact alone should prove that mankind has a mega-malfunction in his nature," (Faith For Earth's Final Hour). During this period, peace is removed by the on-going tension between nations rising against nations as they seek power to dominate in the world. Humanity continues to trust in man-made solutions to peace and all are doomed to collapse and defeat. The promised peace of the white horse rider (Antichrist) is taken away by the red horse rider. The only lasting peace this world will ever know will come from the one known as the **"Prince of Peace" (Isaiah 9:6).** We read, **"and that men would slay one another."** This rider causes men to kill one another. This speaks of lawlessness, rebellion, and revolution where people riot and turn on one another. This is the result of lawlessness and anarchy. We're seeing signs of these things in the world today. Civil strife, racism, terrorism, bombings and all sorts of lawlessness are happening world-wide. During this period, the magnitude, scope, and intensity of these things are escalated. Paul spoke of these times with these words, **"For the mystery of lawlessness is already at work; only he who now restrains will do so until he is taken out of the way" (2 Thessalonians 2:7).** We realize that lawlessness is already a part of our society. However, it's still a mystery in that it has not been fully revealed! When the lawless one, the Antichrist arrives, lawlessness will be fully revealed.

"When He broke the third seal, I heard the third living creature saying, "Come." So I looked, and behold, a

black horse; and he who sat on it had a pair of scales in his hand. And I heard something like a voice in the center of the four living creatures saying, "A quart of wheat for a denarius, and three quarts of barley for a denarius; and do not damage the oil and the wine" (Revelation 6:5-6). This passage speaks of world-wide famine. Famine is shown by the black horse rider having **"a pair of scales in his hand."** The scales symbolize the careful rationing out of the scarce and restricted quantities of food in the world. This also speaks of domination and control over the world by controlling the food supply.

"When the Lamb broke the fourth seal, I heard the voice of the fourth living creature saying, "Come." I looked and behold, an ashen horse; and he who sat on it had the name Death; and Hades was following with him. Authority was given to them over a fourth of the earth, to kill with sword and with famine and with pestilence and by the wild beasts of the earth" (Revelation 6:7-8). This is death on an exceptionally large scale!

The color of this horse speaks volumes. John called the color of this horse **"ashen."** The color of ashen is a pale or yellowish green. In the Greek, it denotes a yellowish green as that of a light green plant (Revelation 9:4), or the paleness of someone who is critically sick or deceased. **In other words, ashen speaks of death and dying.** What does the phrase, **"and he who sat on it had the name Death; and Hades was following with him"** mean? In the Bible, death is described as a separation. In physical death, the soul separates from the body. The body is buried but the soul goes to a particular destination. In this passage, we're told that Hades was following death. In other words, as these people died, Hades was there to claim their souls. According to Luke 16:23, Hades is the destination of souls that do not know Jesus as Savior! The rich man who died without Jesus was in this place called Hades. The place called Hades contains the souls of unbelievers between their death and the time of the Great White Throne Judgment. The Great White Throne Judgment is covered more fully in another chapter of this book. John says, **"Authority was given to them over a fourth of the earth."**

According to the International Census, as of the writing of this book, the world's population stood at 7.3 billion people. One fourth of 7.3 billion is almost 2 billion people! That's a staggering amount of people! This judgment emphasizes death on a huge scale. **We're talking about almost 2 billion people being removed from the earth through this judgment.** This type of destruction of human life is unprecedented! This is the number of people who will die because of the breaking of the 2nd, 3rd, and 4th seals. The unprecedented nature of the tribulation is seen in the description of these horses and their riders.

"When the Lamb broke the fifth seal, I saw underneath the altar the souls of those who had been slain because of the Word of God, and because of the testimony which they had maintained; and they cried out with a loud voice, saying "How long, O Lord, holy and true, will You refrain from judging and revenging our blood on those who dwell on the earth? And there was given to each of them a white robe; and they were told that they should rest for a little while longer, until the number of their fellow servants and their brethren who were to be

killed even as they had been, would be completed also" (Revelation 6:9-11).

Tribulation Martyrs

In this passage, John sees an altar of sacrifice to God. Notice that they were martyred **"because of the Word of God."** During this time of humanity, the human viewpoint is king and any notion of God is rejected. Any person who holds to the Word of God will be persecuted and many will be murdered. The words, **"and because of the testimony which they had maintained,"** speaks to the witness of these who were saved during the tribulation. They persisted and continued their witness even under the persecutions which eventually lead to their being killed. These believers had been slain for their faith in the Lamb of God. John did not see these martyrs in their resurrected bodies **"the souls of those"** because their resurrection comes later. This is covered in Revelation 20:4. These martyrs are alive! Praise God forevermore!

Man, can destroy the body, but no man can kill the soul. Luke 12:4-5 says, **"I say to you, My friends, do not be afraid of those who kill the body and after that have no more that they can do. But I will warn you of whom to fear: fear the One who, after He has killed, has authority to cast in hell; yes, I tell you, fear Him!"** What strength and comfort these words bring to all who may be called to martyrdom! The martyrs ask, **"how long will You refrain from judging." Judging is in reference to "pronounce judgment."** Paul reminds us in the epistle to the Romans, **"Never take your own revenge, beloved, but leave room for the wrath of God, for it is written, 'Vengeance Is Mine, I Will Repay,' says the Lord"** (Romans 12:19).

These martyrs are acting on this promise! They are asking God to bring justice for what happened to them. This is really a cry for God's justice and righteousness to prevail in the earth. **"And there was given to each of them a white robe."** The term **"white robe"** symbolizes the gift of righteousness that was credited to their account because of their belief in Jesus as Lord and Savior. It also symbolizes holiness and purity. We see this in the words of Jesus to the church at Sardis, **"But you have a few people in Sardis who have not soiled their garments; and they will walk with Me in white, for they are worthy. He who overcomes will thus be clothed in white garments; and I will not erase his name from the book of life, and I will confess his name before My Father and before His angels" (Revelation 3:4-5).** These martyrs are clothed in the righteousness of God as followers of Christ! The martyrs are told **"that they should rest for a little while longer."** They are now in the presence of God and the Lamb. They are encouraged to rest and leave matters in the hands of the sovereign God because justice will soon take place. The phrase **"a little while longer"** is in reference to the remaining time of the tribulation.

The duration of the entire tribulation is 7 years. John mentions the phrase **"Until the number of their fellow servants and their brethren who were to be killed even as they had been, would be completed also."** During this time, more people will experience martyrdom on behalf of their Lord Jesus and as evidence of their loving allegiance to Christ! The phrase **"completed also"** reminds us of God's purpose in the deaths of these martyrs. Their deaths do not go unnoticed by God or without His care or control. John does not give us the exact numbers that will cause completion of fulfillment. The exact numbers are known to

God and they're according to His purpose. What we do know are these words of the Psalmist, **"Precious in the sight of the Lord is the death of His godly ones" (Psalm 116:15).** Praise the Lord!

Are you one of His godly ones? Your death can be precious in the sight of the Lord. Just believe that what Jesus did on the cross was for you and begin to live in the light of that fact.

"I looked when He broke the sixth seal, and there was a great earthquake; and the sun became as sackcloth made of hair, and the whole moon became like blood; and the stars of the sky fell to the earth, as a fig casts its unripe figs when shaken by a great wind. The sky was split apart like a scroll when it is rolled up, and every mountain and island were moved out of their places. The kings of the earth and the great men and the commanders and the rich and the strong and every slave and free man hid themselves in the caves and among the rocks of the mountains; and they said to the mountains and to the rocks, "Fall on us and hide us from the presence of Him who sits on the throne, and from the wrath of the Lamb; for the great day of their wrath has come, and who is able to stand" (Revelation 6:12-17).

The previous seal judgments were primarily those that were brought about by the actions of man being used as the instruments of divine judgment. The breaking of the sixth seal shows a direct intervention of the Creator God disturbing the normal order of His creation. The nature and result of breaking the sixth seal is one that causes the vast array of mankind (from kings to slaves) to acknowledge that the Creator God is driving and controlling history. The magnitude of this earthquake is off the charts! It can't be measured by the Richter Scale! The Richter scale is a numerical scale for expressing the magnitude of an earthquake. The more destructive earthquakes typically have magnitudes between about 5.5 and 8.9. The world has never seen an earthquake of this magnitude! God will shake the earth and all the earth will know that there is a God. This is confirmed by the words, **"hide us from the presence of Him who sits on the throne, and from the wrath of the Lamb."** This earthquake will be the most intense shaking of the earth ever!

From the descriptions given by John we see that this is not just a great shaking of the earth, but literally a shaking of the universe. Jesus spoke of this time with these words, **"But immediately after the tribulation of those days the sun will be darkened, and the moon will not give its light, and the stars will fall from the sky, and the powers of the heavens will be shaken" (Matthew 24:29).** John tells us that this shaking affects the moon, stars and the sky. Jesus said, **"the powers of the heavens will be shaken."** It doesn't get any clearer than that! The devastation of this earthquake is beyond our imagination. Whole continents are being realigned. It's outside of our ability to comprehend. As a pastor, for me, the real tragedy of all this is found in the words, **"hide us from the presence of Him who sits on the throne, and from the wrath of the Lamb."** In the middle of all this devastation and suffering these people refuse to call on God for His protection from these horrific judgments. Instead, they choose not to respond to the wrath of God by calling on Jesus for salvation. How very sad this is. Dear reader, if you have not been born again, you can never see or experience the kingdom of God. Being born again is the greatest need you will ever face in this life! Please, don't leave this world without being reconciled to God. Call on Jesus to save you from your sins. Believe that Jesus died on the cross as your substitute, and God will save you! Thanks for allowing me to share that good news with you!

Chapter Four: Why A Pre-Tribulation Rapture of The Church?

Let's begin by looking at what some advocate and teach concerning the rapture of the church. It's called the Post Tribulation Rapture view. The advocates of this view teach that the church will remain on the earth throughout the entire seven-year tribulation period but then will be raptured to meet the Lord in the air immediately after that period, when He returns in His glorious second coming. The Post Tribulationists believe and teach that after the church meets the Lord in the air, it will return immediately to earth with Him as He continues His descent from heaven and will remain with the Lord on the earth throughout the millennium period. In other words, they believe that the rapture of the church and the coming of the Lord with His angels will take place at the same time, immediately after the great tribulation. In chapter two, we've already seen that the rapture of the church and the coming of the Lord with His angels must be two separate and distinct events, and therefore must take place at two different times. **If the Post Tribulation Rapture view is true, then certain biblical prophecies would go unfulfilled. This presents a serious problem for the Post Tribulation Rapture view.**

To understand this problem, we need to observe the following lines of evidence. **First**, the Scriptures teach that when the rapture of the church happens, all church saints, including all the saved alive on the earth at that time, will take part in it (1 Thessalonians 4:17) and will receive glorified resurrection bodies (1 Corinthians 15:51-53) that will not take place in marriage (Mark 12:25) and will not die (Luke 20:36).

Second, when the rapture of the church takes place, every believer alive on the earth will be made sinlessly perfect like the Lord Jesus Christ (1 John 3:2; 1Corinthians 15:42-44). We will have glorified bodies with no sin nature! How exciting is that? Our struggle with sin will be over!

Third, as we observed in chapter two, all the living unsaved will be taken from the earth in judgment when the Lord comes with His angels. Because of this, there will be no unsaved on the earth to enter the millennial kingdom when it's brought to pass after the Lord comes.

Fourth, the Bible prophesies the birth of children during the millennial kingdom (Jeremiah 30:19-20; Ezekiel 47:22). This indicates that there will be marriage during that period of history.

Fifth, the Bible prophesies that a large host of unsaved rebels will follow the devil in a massive revolt against the rule of the Lord after the end of the millennium (Revelation 20:7-9).

Considering these lines of evidence, let's examine the problem with the Post Tribulation Rapture view.

As noted in point number three, the Bible teaches that all the living unsaved will be taken from the earth in judgment when Jesus comes with His angels. Because of this, there will be no unsaved on the earth to enter the millennial kingdom. In the light of this biblical evidence, if the rapture of the church were to happen when the Lord Jesus comes after the great tribulation, as is taught by the Post Tribulation Rapture, the only people who would enter the millennial kingdom would be the saved with glorified resurrection bodies, all of whom would be sinlessly perfect. This would mean that throughout the entire millennium there would be **No** sin, marriage, birth, death, or unsaved rebels. If this was the truth, it would not be possible for the biblical prophecies noted in points four and five to be fulfilled! If all tribulation believers are raptured and glorified just prior to the establishment of the millennial kingdom; **WHO THEN WILL POPULATE AND PROPAGATE THE KINGDOM?** We've already seen that the Scriptures indicate that the living unbelievers will be judged at the end of the great tribulation and taken away from the earth (Matthew 13:24-43; Matthew 13:47-50; Matthew 24:37-41; Luke 17:26-37). Yet, they also teach that children will be born to believers during the millennium and that these children will be capable of sin and rebellion (Isaiah 65:20; Revelation 20:7-10; Jerimiah 30:19-20; Ezekiel 47:22). Children being born indicates that there's marriage during the millennial kingdom. Clearly this **WILL NOT BE POSSIBLE** if all believers on the earth have been glorified through a Post Tribulational Rapture taking place at the end of the great tribulation! If all those who enter the millennium are sinlessly perfect with glorified bodies, and if there are no births during the millennium, where do the wicked of the millennium come from? Where would the large host of earthly unsaved rebels who follow Satan after the millennium come from? Revelation 20:8 says this wicked host is gathered for war against the Lord and His saints, **"…the number of them is like the sand of the seashore." There must be a believing, unglorified human remnant that will populate and propagate the millennium.** The Post Tribulation Rapture forces the conclusion that all the saved will be taken from the earth at Jesus' coming, and therefore no saved will enter the earthly millennial kingdom. This is **CONTRARY** to the biblical teaching that when Jesus comes with His angels at the end of the great tribulation, all the living saved will be left on the earth to enter the millennial kingdom!

Only a Pretribulation Rapture avoids these insurmountable difficulties. It can be concluded that the problem of fulfillment of biblical prophecies mentioned in this section leads to the conclusion in favor of the Pretribulation Rapture view.

In conclusion, the Pretribulation Rapture view teaches that the prophecies noted in the lines of evidence (sin, deception, marriage, birth of children, and rebellion by the unsaved at the end of the millennial kingdom) **WILL BE FULFILLED!** The Pretribulation Rapture view teaches that after the church has been taken from the earth **BEFORE** the tribulation period begins, these events will take place: At the Lord's coming with His angels **AFTER** the tribulation period, all the living unsaved will be taken from the earth in judgment, and all the tribulation saints who are alive will be left on the earth to enter, populate, and propagate the millennial kingdom.

Because these living tribulation saints never experienced death, they will enter the kingdom in their mortal bodies as well as their sin natures. Because of this, they will be able to have marriage and give birth to children during this time. Those children will be born with sin natures and are unsaved. We must understand that although no unsaved will **ENTER** the millennial kingdom, after time through birth, unsaved people will be present on the earth again. In other words, many of those born during the millennium

WILL NEVER GET SAVED! THIS WILL SET THE STAGE FOR THE SATANIC REBELLION! THE UNSAVED HOST WILL FOLLOW SATAN WHEN HE'S LOOSED FROM IMPRISONMENT AFTER THE MILLENNIUM (Revelation 20:7-9).

Chapter Five: The Relationship of The Church to The Wrath of God

This chapter deals with the question, "Will the church go through or participate in the tribulation?" To answer this question, we must understand some things:

1. **God's purpose for the tribulation.**
2. **Does God's purpose for the tribulation exclude the church?**
3. **What is the nature and purpose of the church?**
4. **By way of review, what is the character and nature of the tribulation?**
5. **Are the Lord's program and plans for Israel different than His program and plans for the church?**

Let's examine the purpose of the tribulation. The phrase **"The tribulation"** refers to a specific event, not a general condition. It's very important that we grasp the distinction. Remember from chapter three, which deals with the tribulation, we said that the word "tribulation" is used in general of any type of testing, distress, or trouble. This testing, distress, or trouble is used to describe what the church experiences in its dealings with this current world system. This is what I mean by using the term tribulation for being a general condition!

However, we've seen that the Bible also uses the word tribulation to refer to **"a specific time of trouble, a special time of judgment from the Lord God."** This is the specific event, and not the general condition! While the Lord warned the disciples that they and every Christ follower would experience tribulation as a general condition in this world (John 16:33; Romans 5:3), He very clearly identified the great tribulation as having a specified beginning and end! It will begin when the **"abomination that causes desolation"** prophesied by Daniel is erected in the temple (in the middle of the last 7 years of this age) and will end just prior to the Lord's second coming in judgment, 3.5 years later (Daniel 9:24-27; Matthew 24:9-15, 29-30).

The great tribulation is primarily Jewish in its focus. It does not focus at all on the church! See part E under the heading of **"the character and nature of the tribulation"** in the chapter on the tribulation. In fact, it was referred to as **"Jacob's Distress"** until the Lord Jesus called it the **"great tribulation"** in Matthew 24:21. In so doing, the Lord Jesus said the "great tribulation" would be a time of unprecedented distress, unique in the history of the world. The passage found in Jeremiah 30:3-11 provides for us the clearest description of its overall purpose. In this passage of Scripture, the event is foretold, its purpose revealed, and the timing is made clear. Let's examine the timing of the event. According to **Jeremiah 30:3**, it will happen after Israel and Judah are re-gathered in the land as one nation, **"For behold, days are coming, declares the Lord, when I will restore the fortunes of My people Israel and Judah. The Lord says, I will also bring them back to the land that I gave to their forefathers and they shall possess it."** Jeremiah 33:9, says it will result in David becoming their King again, **"But they shall serve the Lord their God and David their King, whom I will raise up for them."** We must understand there have been two re-gatherings since that passage of Scripture was penned, but the first, starting in 535 BC, didn't result in David becoming Israel's king! As a matter of fact, from approximately 600 BC to now, the nation of Israel has had no legitimate king at all! See Ezekiel 34:23-24; 37:24-28! In Jeremiah 30:9, we see the phrase **"David their king."** No king of David's seed has held the scepter since the captivity.

The second re-gathering began in 1948 AD and it continues today. Even though the Jewish population of Israel continues to grow, so does the Jewish populations of all the nations to which the Jews were scattered! There are still about as many Jews who are outside of Israel than are in the land. All that will change as the Lord God calls His remnant people to return to their Promised Land. Therefore, it's the second re-gathering that fulfills the passage of Jeremiah 30:3-11. Isaiah prophesied that the second re-gathering of Israel would bring an end to the hostility between Israel and Judah in Isaiah 11:11-13, and Ezekiel confirms that sometime after this reunion David will be their king (Ezekiel 37:15-25), emphasis on verses 24-25.

Let's examine the purpose of the event. It's found in verse 11 of Jeremiah chapter 30. It reads, **"For I am with you, declares the Lord, to save you; For I will destroy completely all the nations where I have scattered you, Only I will not destroy you completely. But I will chasten you justly and will by no means leave you unpunished."** The idea here is that Israel must undergo a period of restoration and conversion for the millennial reign of Jesus that was promised by God. Israel must be purified in preparation for the millennial kingdom of Jesus on the earth. Also, the nations to which Israel was scattered will be destroyed by the Lord. Both events will take place in the tribulation, a time of Jacob's Distress!

We can see that the main purposes of the tribulation are: To discipline or purify the remnant of Israel, and destroy the nations to which Israel had been scattered. None of the purposes has anything to do with the church!

What is the nature of the church? According to apostle Paul, the church is nothing less than a new race of humanity, consisting of both Jews and Gentiles but sharing a destiny with neither. 1 Corinthians 10:32-33 says, **"Give no offense either to Jews or to Greeks or to the church of God; just as I also please all men in all things, not seeking my own profit but the profit of the many, so that they may be saved."** Notice that these three groups represent all humanity; Jews, Greeks, and the church! **No longer being either Jew or Gentile means the tribulation does not fit the purpose of the church.** Remember we saw that God's purpose for the tribulation dealt primarily with the discipline or purifying the people of Israel (Jews), and the complete destruction of the nations (Gentiles) to which the Jews had been scattered, (Jeremiah 30:11). At the cross of Jesus, God reconciled all things to Himself, things in heaven and on earth (Colossians 1:19-20). This means that God was now at peace with His creation for the first time since Adam's rebellion in Eden. God accomplished this by paying the price for the sins of those He's called. Now, for all who would accept it, a full pardon for sins past, present and future was available, free for the asking. Accepting God's pardon qualifies any person, young or old, Jew or Gentile, good or bad, to become a new creation (2 Corinthians 5:17). When this happens, it permits the Lord God to Look upon us as standing in the righteousness of Jesus. **It also requires the division of mankind into three groups: Jew, Gentile and Church (1Corinthians 10:32).** No longer being either Jew or Gentile (Galatians 3:26-28) means that the Lord God's purpose is not served by having the church present in the tribulation!!

I believe it's very critical that we understand and see the Lord's perspective in this because it's totally different from human perspective. To God, the church is without sin, blameless and holy, and has been since the cross of Jesus (Ephesians 5:25-27). Whatever sins we as individuals have committed or will commit have been forgiven (Colossians 2:13-14) and it's as if they never happened (2 Corinthians 5:17). At the cross, the church became the righteousness of God in Christ (2 Corinthians 5:21). Because of the cross of Jesus Christ, God has a people with whom He can live in peace. He has a people that's been reconciled to Him! No further preparation for restoration and conversion is needed for the church. On the cross, Jesus said these words, **"It is finished" or "Paid in full!"** See John 19:30. Because of this, no purpose is served by having the church take part in the tribulation. We must remember that the church is a company of believers covering some 40 generations of human life. If as the church, we were not all declared the righteousness of God in Christ, how could the suffering of the final generation of believers serve to purify all those who have preceded us? All the generations of the church have died in hope of spending eternity with the Lord as the Word of God promises us. Is it only ours who will receive this promise and then only after sharing in Israel's purification? No, of course not!

With Israel, it's a different matter. The past generations of Jews who rejected their Messiah are lost. The last generation's purification through the tribulation will not save those who have gone before. It's intended to finally open their eyes and hearts to the Lord Jesus so that a remnant of God's chosen people can be saved (Zechariah 12:10-13).

As we have seen, during the time called the tribulation, God's focus will be on Israel and His focus is always either Israel or the church, never both at once (Acts 15:12-18 and Romans 11:25-27).

Summation: We've seen that the Word of God promises that the church will not be present on earth during any part of the tribulation. The tribulation is not God's purpose for the church. The church is regarded as a company of believers distinct from Israel and from Israel's program and promises! **It seems most logical to believe that God's program for the church will be finished before God resumes His announced program for Israel and the Gentiles in the tribulation. The removal of the church from the earth ends God's program for His church.** In confirmation of this, there's no reference to the church in any of the many tribulation passages. Therefore, the church's presence on earth during the tribulation period would serve no purpose and in fact would be in direct opposition to our nature as the Lord God sees us. It is also in direct opposition to the nature of God that's revealed in the Scriptures. Do you recall the basis of Abraham's prayer to God concerning the destruction of the cities of Sodom and Gomorrah? The passage is found in Genesis 18:23-25. In verse 23, Abraham said to the Lord, **"Will You indeed sweep away the righteous with the wicked?"**

Abraham used this negotiation with God in verses 23, 24, 25, 28, 29, 30, 31 and 32! God knows how to remove the church from the time, place, and cause of the coming judgment before unleashing it upon the world. He does so through the rapture (Romans 5:9; 1 Thessalonians 1:10; 1 Thessalonians 5:9; Revelation 3:10).

A Closer Look at Revelation 3:10

The text says, **"Because you have kept the word of My perseverance, I also will keep you from the hour of testing, that hour which is about to come upon the whole world, to test those who dwell on the earth."** In this passage of Scripture, we're given the biblical teaching concerning the relationship of the church to the wrath of God. The Lord Jesus Christ is making this promise to the church in Philadelphia and understanding the significance of this promise requires careful exegesis. The phrase **"the word of My perseverance"** refers to the Word, the testimony of Scripture concerning the truth of who Jesus is as the suffering, resurrected and the victorious Savior who endured the shame of rejection and the cross and who endures today as the resurrected and ascended Lord. The word **"kept"** is the Greek word translated "to guard, keep, watch over, protect" or "obey, observe" as with the commands and principles of the Bible. The word "kept" is a non-motion verb and stands in contrast to the verbs of motion such as, "to deliver, rescue, or save." **In other words, we're not going to be delivered out of anything, but kept from it!** It's important to stress this fact because this same word is used of the promise which follows. When we consider the promise, we'll see why. What does it mean **"you have kept the word of My perseverance?"** It means to be a Christ follower, one who has put his trust in the person and work of the Lord Jesus Christ. Rather than rejecting this message, these Christ followers kept it by faith. Let's examine the phrase, **"I also will keep you from the hour of testing."** The word **"testing"** is the Greek word translated "a trial, testing, or temptation." We must allow the context to determine the precise meaning of the word. In this passage, the context shows us the reference is to a very specific meaning, that of world-wide testing or tribulation. **The context shows that this word "testing" is in reference to testing or trying people to determine, expose or demonstrate the kind of people they are. In other words, as Christ followers, they were already exposed to have been people who kept God's commands.** The word **"hour"** is a metaphor describing a shortened period. It is to come upon the whole world. The Greek word translated **"world"** means "the inhabited earth," but it's modified by the adjective **"whole."** In other words, the testing is worldwide! Jesus was referring to a period when the entire inhabited earth will be tested. He was not talking about unrelated incidents of testing, widely separated from each other in time and location and therefore never worldwide in scope (general versus specific). **Jesus was talking about a specific, distinct future period that will be uniquely characterized by its intense, concentrated, worldwide scope of testing. We know this to be the tribulation period!** Lastly, it is designed to test a specific category of people described as **"those who dwell on the earth."** The word **"dwell"** means to inhabit. The construction of the Greek describes the inhabitants as those who are characterized as **"earth dwellers."** As used in the Book of Revelation, it is a term for "unbelievers," because they are seen as people who are bound only to this life and what this life can give. See

Revelation 6:10; 8:13; 11:10; 13:8; 14; 17:8 and Isaiah 24:17. **In contrast to Christ followers who are to have the mindset and live as "strangers, aliens or sojourners," the "earth dwellers" are quite at home on earth.** With respect to the identification of "earth dwellers," a careful examination of all the references to them in Revelation clearly indicates that they will be those who, during the tribulation, will kill the saints of God (Revelation 6:10); thereby, they'll be haters of the saints of the Lord. Notice the passage in Revelation 6:10. It says, **"And they cried out with a loud voice, saying, 'How long, O Lord, holy and true, will you refrain from judging and avenging our blood on those who dwell on the earth?'"** In Revelation 11:10 we read, **"And those who dwell on the earth will rejoice over them and celebrate; and they will send gifts to one another, because these two prophets tormented those who dwell on the earth."** Once again, we're shown the nature of the "earth dwellers" and the fact that they are unbelievers and haters of the saints of the Lord. Here they're identified as despising the two witnesses of God by celebrating their deaths. It's also interesting to take note of the fact that the Greek word translated **"tormented"** means to "test the genuineness of," showing that the activities of the two witnesses is one aspect of how God will test those dwelling on the earth during the tribulation, Daniel's 70th Week, Jacob's Distress. **Every reference of these "earth dwellers" in Revelation clearly reveals that these people are the unsaved of the future period of testing, who never get saved.**

The Promise For The Church

First, we need to recognize that the promise is not a reward to the faithful. This will come later in Revelation 3:11-12. Instead, this is a promise to the church. This is confirmed by the words of Revelation 3:13 which says, **"He who has an ear, let him hear what the Spirit says to the churches."** Verse 13 broadens this as a promise to the churches at large. In other words, all believers are to heed these messages and their warning, and act in accordance with them. This promise is designed to bring comfort and exhortation to the church.

Now let's continue our exegesis of the promise by looking at the phrase, **"I also will keep you from the hour,"** (the tribulation). This phrase is very specific and carefully described in the Greek to clearly emphasize and teach the Pretribulation Rapture of the Church. The Greek word translated **"from"** in the expression **"from the hour"** is important to understand. It carries the sense of separation from a thing or person. **In other words, the Lord Jesus promised to keep the church separated from the hour of testing. Praise the Lord forevermore!** The Lord Jesus Christ will separate the church from the hour of testing by removing it from the earth before that period begins! How do we know? First, the Lord Jesus promised to separate the church from the period of testing, not from the testing only. This means that Jesus will separate the church from the entire period of testing. **The only way to keep the church from an entire period of testing is to prevent the church from ever entering that period!** The only people who'll enter this period are those present on the earth (Jews and Gentiles). **The only way to prevent people from entering the whole period of testing is to remove them from the earth before the time ever began. This is what the rapture of the church does!** Also, the Lord Jesus based

90

His promise on the fact that the testing would be for those "who dwell on the earth" or unbelievers! The testing which is to come has not been designed for the Christ follower but for the "earth dwellers!" The period of testing for the Christ follower has been fulfilled by the words of Jesus which says, **"Because you have kept the word of My perseverance..."** (James 1:2-4, 12; Romans 5:1-5). Notice that the Lord followed His promise of keeping the church out of the hour of testing with these words, **"I am coming quickly.,"** (Revelation 3:11). This expression speaks of Jesus' "imminent" return. It means "suddenly, without announcement." It implies imminence so we're told to **"hold fast"** which warns us against spiritual carelessness and carnality. The warning is a reminder to the church to live in the light of our Lord's coming! In other words, until the Lord's imminent return becomes a past event, the tribulation period is always a future event! Every time people have said to me, "We're already in the tribulation," I always respond, "That's not possible because the church is still here!" As the church, we will experience tribulation, but we will not experience the tribulation!

Chapter Six: Imminence and The Rapture of The Church

A. The Doctrine of Imminence
   a. **Imminence Defined**
      i. "Near"
      ii. "Close at hand"
      iii. "Approaching"
      iv. "To move or become nearer in frame to something" in the sense that it could occur at any moment.
      v. Other things **MAY** occur prior to the event, but nothing else **MUST** happen before the event occurs. In other words, if something else **MUST** happen before an event can happen, then that event is not imminent. If something **MUST** happen first before an event, the idea of imminence is destroyed! I once heard a Word of Faith teacher say, "God is not going to come back for a church that's poor." His teaching was that the church needed to be rich before the Lord would come for it! The teaching not only is false and unsound, but with that statement, he destroyed the concept of imminence! He stated that the church **MUST** be rich before the Lord could come

back! This is not what the Bible teaches with respect to the rapture of the church!

> **vi.** When an event or occurrence is imminent, one never knows exactly when it will take place. In his book "Our Lord's Second Coming as a Motive to World-Wide Evangelism," A. T. Pierson noted, "Imminence is the combination of two conditions viz, certainly and uncertainty. By an imminent event we mean one which is certain to occur at some time, uncertain at what time."

> **vii.** Why is imminence important? The doctrine of imminence is significant because of the motivation it provides for Christ followers to purify their lives and press onward to the goal of sanctification and Christlikeness! Remember, **All** doctrine is practical!

b. Descriptions of Imminence

Because one never knows exactly when an imminent event will take place, the following statements are true.

> **i.** One can't count on a certain amount of time transpiring before the imminent event happens. Because of this, one should **ALWAYS BE PREPARED** for it to take place **AT ANY MOMENT**.

> **ii.** One can't set a date for an imminent event to take place. As soon as a

date is set for an imminent event to take place, imminence is ruined. Setting dates means that a certain amount of time must transpire before that event can take place. In other words, a set date is in opposition to imminence!

The Coming of Christ Is an Imminent Event

1. Jesus' coming to rapture the church is near.
2. Jesus' coming to rapture the church is close at hand.
3. Jesus' coming to rapture the church is close at hand in the sense that it could take place at any moment.
4. Other things **MAY** occur prior to the rapture, but nothing else **MUST** happen before the rapture happens. If something else **MUST** happen before Jesus can come for the church, then His coming for the church is not imminent. If something else **MUST** happen before Jesus can come for the church, imminence is ruined.
5. Since the Lord's coming for the church is imminent, Christ followers will never know exactly when Christ will come.

Is the doctrine of imminence found in Scripture? J. G. Davies, the Edward Cadbury Professor of Theology at the University of Birmingham, stated that the expectation of Christ's **imminent coming** is "so vivid in the New

Testament.," "The Early Christian Church." J. Barton Payne declared, "In fact, no natural reading of Scripture would produce any other conclusion, "The Imminent Appearing of Christ."

A. **(1 Corinthians 16:22)** "Maranatha"
   1. Its meaning. The word **"Maranatha"** derives from three Aramaic words: "Mar" (Lord), "ana" (our), and "tha" (come). Thus, the whole term meant "our Lord come." (Leon Morris, "The First Epistle of Paul To the Corinthians").
   2. Its form. The word "Maranatha" had the form of a petition. "erchomai," (Strong's Exhaustive Concordance of The Bible, 2001, p. 1625).

Origin and importance. Leon Morris comments that Maranatha being Aramaic…. cannot have originated among the Greeks, but must go back to the early days of the church in Palestine. Moreover, it must have expressed a sentiment that the early church regarded as very important, else, the foreign word would never have been taken over in this way by Greek-speaking Christians. ("The First Epistle of Paul To the Corinthians") p. 247. Renald Showers in his book "Maranatha Our Lord Come!" p. 131 states: It would appear, then, that the fixed usage of the term "Maranatha" by the early Christians was a witness to their strong belief in the imminent return of Christ. If they knew that He could not return at any moment because of other events or a time which had to transpire first, then why did they petition Him in a way that implied that He could come at any moment."

(James 5:7-9) In his book, "Maranatha: Our Lord, Come" R. Showers says, "The important thing to note about James 5:7-9 is the fact that the Greek verbs translated "is near" (v8) and "standing" (v9) are in the perfect tense and in the indicative mood, meaning that each of these verbs refers to an action that was completed before James wrote his epistle and that continues on in that completed state." (H. E. Dana and Julius R. Mantley, A Manual Grammar of the Greek New Testament), p. 200. The implication is that Christ's coming drew near before James wrote his epistle, and His coming continues to be near. In addition, Christ as judge began to stand before the door before James wrote his epistle, and Christ as judge continues to stand before the door. In other words, Christ's coming was imminent. James wanted to impress his readers with the fact that Christ could come through the door at any moment and cause them as Christ followers to stand before Him at the Judgment Seat of Christ. He could do so today! The Lord's coming for His church is described as **"near"** and as **"standing right at the door."** Both phrases speak of an event that could take place at any moment! The passage in James 5:7-9 speaks of Jesus' coming as an imminent event. For the Christ follower, realizing that the Lord could step through the door and appear for them at any moment is designed to bring comfort and encouragement as well as motivation for Christlikeness! Both of these texts and many more, suggests that in the early church, expectation of the Lord's return ran high. A firm persuasion that Jesus could return at any moment saturates the New Testament! The apostle Paul said it best with these words **"For the grace of God has appeared, bringing salvation to all men, instructing us to deny ungodliness, and worldly desires and to live sensibly, righteously and godly in the**

present age, looking for the blessed hope and the appearing of the glory of our great God and Savior, Christ Jesus" (Titus 2:11-13). Notice the event that's described as our hope is **"the appearing of the glory which belongs to Jesus Christ as God and Savior."** Most assuredly, Christ followers will see and experience that glory in the Lord when He comes to rapture the church. Since our Lord's appearing is an event that we're told to **"look for"** it must be defined as an event that could happen at any moment!

The Judgment: (Matthew 25:31-33)

The Sheep: (Matthew 25:34-40)

The Goats: (Matthew 25:41-46)

The significance of this judgment is that it brings an end to the times of the Gentiles. God in His sovereignty has allowed Gentile nations to assume great power, especially with respect to the nation of Israel.

The details of this judgment are as follows:

The context shows that this judgment takes place at the second coming of Christ to the earth, preceding the establishment of His earthly millennial kingdom. This is seen in the words, **"But when the Son of Man comes in glory, and all the angels with Him" (Matthew 25:31).** At the second coming of Christ there will be a series of judgments. A similar judgment of Israel is spoken of by the prophet Ezekiel in 20:33-38. Those found worthy will enter the millennial kingdom. Those not counted worthy are put to death. The sheep and goat judgment, therefore, is to be distinguished in time from all other judgments i.e., the tribulation judgments or the great white throne judgment.

The sheep and goat judgment follows the second coming of the Lord Jesus Christ to earth and is a preparation for His 1000-year reign on earth. Where is the place of the judgment? This can be answered from our text. The phrase, **"the Son of Man comes in glory, and all the angels with Him,"** is a picture of Jesus Christ and the angels coming from heaven to earth! This is confirmed by another time phrase, **"Then He will sit on His glorious throne."** This is not about the throne of God in heaven, but the earthly throne spoken of by the prophets. Jeremiah said, **"Behold, the days are coming, declares the Lord, when I will raise up for David a righteous Branch; and He will reign as king and act wisely and do justice and righteousness in the land" (Jeremiah 23:5).** The place of the sheep and goat judgment, therefore, is not heaven but the millennial earth.

The Subjects of the Judgment

In our text **(Matthew 25:32),** the subjects of this divine judgment are clearly said to be **"all nations."** The Greek word for "nations" is ethne. It is a common word in the Word of God and generally used to describe non-Jewish races. In other words, in this passage, the word **"all nations" is translated "all Gentiles."** This judgment deals with the Gentiles or the non-Jewish population of the world. This is also confirmed by the fact that in our passage the phrase **"all the nations"** is contrasted with the phrase **"these brothers of Mine" (Matthew 25:40).** As mentioned earlier, a similar judgment comes to the Jewish people (Ezekiel 20:33-38) and the sheep and goat judgment refers to Gentiles only! This judgment is the ending of the reign of Gentile nations, more specifically, all Gentiles who have survived the great tribulation. Those deemed worthy are described as sheep and they will enter the millennial kingdom of Christ. Those deemed not worthy are described as goats and are put to death. They'll be taken away from the earth in death (judgment).

The Basis of the Judgment

According to the Bible, as all gentiles are gathered before the Lord for judgment, they're divided into two groups. One group is called **"sheep"** and the other is called **"goats."** We read**, "And He will put the sheep on His right, and the goats on the left" (Matthew 25:33).** After making this separation, the Lord explains what He's doing by addressing the sheep. Jesus as "the King" says to the sheep on His right: **"Come, you who are blessed of My Father, inherit the kingdom prepared for you from the foundation of the world. For I was hungry, and you gave Me to eat; I was thirsty, and you gave Me to drink; I was a stranger, and you invited Me in; naked, and you clothed Me; I was sick, and you visited Me; I was in prison, and you came to Me" (Matthew 25:34-36).** The words spoken by Jesus are deserving of attention because they describe ordinary works such as feeding those who are hungry, providing drink for those who are thirsty, clothing the naked, visiting the sick and those who are in prison. Also, the Lord declares that they who have done these things have done them to Him personally! The righteous answer Him with the question, **"Lord, when did we see You hungry, and feed You, or thirsty, and give You to drink? And when did we see You a stranger, and invite You in, or naked, and clothe You? When did we see You sick, or in prison, and come to You?" (Matthew 25:37-39).** As "the King" Jesus replies, **"Truly I say to you, to the extent that you did it to one of these brothers of Mine, even the least of them, you did it to Me" (Matthew 25:40).**

In contrast to this, Jesus then turns to those on the left described as goats and says, **"Depart from Me , accursed ones, into the eternal fire which has been prepared for the devil and his angels; for I was hungry, and you gave**

Me nothing to eat; I was thirsty, and you gave Me nothing to drink; I was a stranger, and you did not invite Me in; naked, and you did not clothe Me; sick, and in prison, and you did not visit Me," (Matthew 25:41-43). In the same manner, the goats replied asking when they had neglected these works of kindness (Matthew 25:44). The goats are judged by the Lord with these words, "Truly I say to you, to the extent that you did not do it to one of the least of these, you did not do it to Me. These will go away into eternal punishment, but the righteous into eternal life" (Matthew 25:45-46). Let me say that this passage has troubled many for it seems to indicate that the sheep go into eternal life due to their righteous works while the goats are condemned for their lack of righteous works. Some wrongly interpret this passage to mean that a person can be saved by their works. However, when other passages are brought to bear concerning salvation by works, it becomes very clear that salvation by works is not possible under any circumstances! The Bible teaches that all people are spiritually dead and no amount of good works can reverse the sentence of death or change the sinful nature of mankind. Works can never, ever be the basis of a person's salvation! There is no cure for the sinner other than God's amazing grace that was displayed on the cross of Jesus Christ! Even though works are never the basis of salvation, they can be the evidence of it. A person who is saved will show the evidence of that salvation! Apostle James said, "But are you willing to recognize, you foolish fellow, that faith without works is useless?" (James 2:20). The faith that James is talking about is saving faith or faith that leads to salvation. It was Abraham's offering of Isaac that demonstrated the genuineness of his faith in God and the reality of his justification before God. This is shown in James 2:21. James is not teaching that a person is saved by works. He's teaching that a person who is saved will have corresponding works because of that saving faith. Our passage in **Matthew 25:31-46** emphasizes the significance of works, not as the basis for salvation, but as evidence or proof of it! Let's continue our examination of the text. We must know something about the circumstances which form the background of the sheep and goat judgment. The Gentiles being judged are those who have survived the devastation and horrors of the tribulation. During this period, anti-Semitism will be extremely high. This is evidenced by the words of Jeremiah, **"the time of Jacob's trouble" (Jeremiah 30:7).** It's also evident from Jesus' warning that the Jewish people will be harassed and relentlessly persecuted during the tribulation **(Matthew 24:15-22).** In other words, satanic hatred of the Jewish people will be shown to such a degree as have never been. This hatred will be part of the world-wide deception which causes men to believe a lie. Paul tells us about this period with these words, **"God will send upon them a deluding influence so that they will believe what is false, in order that they may be judged who did not believe the truth, but took pleasure in wickedness" (2 Thessalonians 2:11-12).** Under these circumstances, combined with the satanic hatred of God as well as the compulsion to worship the Antichrist (the beast of Revelation 13), any person that would befriend a Jewish person would certainly be marked for death. In this period of universal hatred of Jews, one who befriends Jews will by this work or evidence manifest his salvation! In other words, for a Gentile to befriend one that Jesus called **"these brothers of Mine"** would be outstanding and will be motivated by a realization that the

Jewish people are the people of God and that Christ is the Savior of all who follow Him. These Gentiles are identified as **"sheep."** Befriending the Jewish people during this period will be acts of kindness that results from Gentiles who are saved! The goats that followed the world system, the beast and the false prophet, in its participation of persecuting the Jewish people now face the awful judgment which they justly deserve, and are thrown into everlasting fire.

The Judgment

The purpose of the Gentile judgment is one of separating the righteous from the unrighteous in preparation for the millennial kingdom of Christ. This is the fulfillment of Jesus' teachings on the parable of the wheat and tares **(Matthew 13:24-46),** and His teaching on the parable of the dragnet **(Matthew 13:47-50).** These Gentiles will enter the millennial kingdom in their natural, unglorified bodies. They still have a natural life to live, as well as helping to populate the millennial kingdom. The tossing of the goats into everlasting fire is not their final judgment. Their final judgment comes after the millennial kingdom, when they'll stand before the great white throne Judgment. Although the goats will move into divine judgment at the start of the millennial kingdom, it will be in Hades, the temporary abode of the wicked dead. Their judgment in the passage of **Matthew 25:31-46** is that they're put to death physically, but still subject to the second death at the great white throne (Revelation 20:5-6, 11-15). The sheep and goat judgment ends the times of the Gentiles (Luke 21:24).

Chapter Eight: The Second Coming of Christ

Our passage of Scripture is found in Revelation 19:11-21. This section outlines the return of Christ as **"King of kings, and Lord of lords."** In this passage of the Bible, we arrive at a climactic place as it reveals the person of the Lord Jesus Christ as the Victorious White Horse Rider who comes from heaven as the King of kings and Lord of lords! The gospel accounts of Jesus which primarily deal with Jesus' first coming, show Him in His humiliation, rejection, suffering, death, resurrection, and ascension. Here, we're shown that His second coming is one of power, glory, triumph, sovereignty and dominion! We're shown the high point in history, for here is the manifestation of God the Son in glory, to bring an end to the reign of the beast and false prophet, and the destruction of their armies (Revelation 20:19-20). The Lord comes to end the Battle of Armageddon. Here the program of God is climaxed. God exalts His Son and puts all creation under His feet, a symbol of His dominance and control (Psalm 2; Ephesians 1:22; Hebrews 1:13; Psalm 110:1).

Let's examine our text. John writes, **"And I saw heaven opened, and behold, a white horse, and He who sat on it is called Faithful and True, and in righteousness He judges and wages war" (Revelation 19:11).**

The One who ascended to heaven (Acts 1:9-11) and had been seated at the right hand of the Father (Ephesians 1:20-21) will return to take back the earth from the rule of Satan and establish His kingdom (Revelation 5:1-10). The nature of this event (the second coming) shows how it's distinct from the rapture of the church. During the rapture, Jesus meets His church in the air. In this event, Jesus comes with His church to the earth. At the rapture, there's no judgment. At this event, it's all judgment. The Savior arrives on a white horse followed by His armies (the church and God's angels). The phrase, **"and behold, a white horse, and He who sat on it"** is not the white horse rider of Revelation 6:2. That white horse rider is the Antichrist, the beast of Revelation 13:1-10, who brings new levels of chaos and evil to the earth. This white horse rider comes to vanquish that evil! The rider of Revelation 6:2 had a crown that **"was given to him."** This crown speaks not of royalty but of a laurel wreath. The rider of Revelation 6:2 becomes king, chosen by the inhabitants of the world. The rider of Revelation 19:12 has **"on His head many diadems."** The diadem is the crown of royalty! When the Lord was crucified, they gave Him a crown of thorns (Matthew 27:29; Mark 15:17; John 19:2, 5). It was given as an attempt to mock royalty. To the Christ follower, however, it testified of His true kingship, and it pointed forward to His victory over death and His return as King of kings. John says, **"He who sat on it is called Faithful and True."** This phrase describes a name used of our Savior and to His person and work.

"Faithful" refers to "one you can always rely on." This wonderful characteristic of the King of kings flows out of His divine nature and perfect, glorified manhood. **Remember, Jesus is 100% Man and 100% God!** Concerning Jesus, Paul said, **"In whom are hidden all the treasures of wisdom and knowledge" (Colossians 2:3).** Paul also said about Jesus, **"For in Him all the fullness of Deity dwells in bodily form" (Colossians 2:9).** These attributes can't be said about any other person! Other rulers, due to their ignorance or lack of wisdom continue to show themselves untrustworthy and fail those that follow. But this Man possesses all wisdom and knowledge! His knowledge and wisdom can't change, nor be mistaken. Jesus is trustworthy. Jesus is reliable. You can depend on Jesus. Jesus is called **"True."** In John's gospel, Jesus said, "I am the truth" (John 14:6). This word "true" means "real, genuine as opposed to false." **Jesus is the "real deal."** This word **"true"** also means the "ideal" as opposed to the imperfect." **Humanity has long desired the perfect ruler, one who possessed the power, authority, love, grace, wisdom, holiness, and the ability to rule in perfect righteousness! Look no further! His name is Jesus!** The phrase, **"and in righteousness He judges and wages war"** speaks about the purpose of the Lord's second coming. The phrase **"in righteousness"** means "by means of." It emphasizes that what follows is the result of the perfect righteousness of Christ Jesus! In other words, all evil and the enemies of God are about to be executed and removed from the earth. It's getting ready to go down! The words, **"judges" and "wages war"** are in the present tense and are used to describe the process. Once it begins, it won't end until every enemy of God that has stood in rebellion and hatred against God is judged and taken away through death. On the cross, the Lord defeated Satan and set in motion his final defeat. Paul said it best with these words, **"For the word of the cross is foolishness to those who are perishing, but to us who are being saved it is the power of God" (1 Corinthians 1:18).** Here, at the second coming, Satan's defeat is carried out. **"His eyes are a flame of fire, and on His head, are many diadems; and He has a name written on Him which no one knows**

except Himself" (Revelation 19:12). The phrase **"His eyes are a flame of fire"** speaks of the Lord's ability to see past all pretenses. Absolutely nothing is hidden from His penetrating gaze. The eyes of Christ search and understand all things. This phrase indicates the ability of Christ to penetrate all disguises and to judge things as they are, not as they might pretend to be. Jesus sees the heart and examines all things according to the perfect standard of His holiness. John added that Jesus **"has a name written on Him which no one knows except Himself."** We must keep in mind that we're talking about the Triune God, Jesus Christ. There certainly are unfathomable mysteries within the Godhead (Father, Son, and Holy Spirit) that the human mind is not able to comprehend.

"He is clothed with a robe dipped in blood, and His name is called The Word of God" (Revelation 19:13). Either in His own blood by which He is Savior of the church, or else in the blood of the saints, He comes now to avenge, or rather in the blood of His enemies, with which He appears, as stained, before the battle is fought, the victory being sure, and their slaughter unavoidable. The metaphor **"dipped in blood"** is taken from persons treading in a winepress, whose garments are stained from the fresh juice of stomped grapes. See the passage in Revelation 14:18-20. **"And His name is called The Word of God."** For the Christ follower, this is the name we should know with certainty and conviction. If forced to choose the one endeavor of my life as a Christ follower over any others, I without hesitation, would choose the reading and study of the Word of God! If a Christ follower is committed to the Word of God, he or she will become a person that will worship God, mature in their relationship with God, serve in the local place of worship, fellowship with other Christ followers, and be involved in telling others about Jesus. It's the Word of God believed and applied that brings godly change to our lives. Paul tells us, **"For this reason we also constantly thank God that when you received the word of God which you heard from us, you accepted it not as the word of men, but for what it really is, the word of God, which also performs its work in you who believe" (1 Thessalonians 2:13).**

"And the armies which are in heaven, clothed in fine linen, white and clean, were following Him on white horses" (Revelation 19:14). We've seen many passages that show that angels accompany Jesus at His second coming (Matthew 13:24-30, 47-50; 24:37-41; Luke 17:26-37). The angels are part of this army. Also, the church is seen coming back with Jesus from heaven. The church is part of this army. All the tribulation martyrs and the Old Testament saints are part of this coming with the Lord. They are part of this army from heaven. According to Revelation 17:14, the Lamb goes to war with an army that's identified as **"the called and chosen and faithful."** John says they are **"clothed in fine line, white and clean."** John tells us in Revelation 19:8 that the **"fine linen is the righteous acts of the holy ones."**

"From His mouth comes a sharp sword, so that with it He may strike down the nations, and He will rule them with a rod of iron; and He treads the winepress of the fierce wrath of God, the Almighty" (Revelation 19:15). The Lord Jesus will smite His enemies with His Word, that's symbolized by **"a sharp sword."** As King of kings, Jesus will execute **"the fierce wrath of God"** on His enemies. The authority of Jesus is on display as He smites the nations in judgment, slaying and removing them from the earth. This is in preparation for the millennial kingdom. During this time, Jesus will **"rule them with a rod of iron."** In other words, no lawlessness or injustices are allowed. People today can get away with injustices, but not during this time! The Lord's authority is further seen by the phrase **"and he treads the winepress of the fierce wrath of God, the Almighty."** This phrase speaks of what Jesus must do to take up His rule on earth. It's a devastating picture of judgment that happens at His second coming (Revelation 14:19-20). The image is that of treading a winepress that's full of grapes. The press runs red with the juice from the grapes which have been pulverized by the treading. This judgment speaks of a bloodbath! The armies of the Antichrist will be wiped out, taken away in judgment.

"And on His robe and on His thigh, He has a name written, "KING OF KINGS, AND LORD OF LORDS" (Revelation 19:16). This name emphasizes the absolute authority over all human rulers! Jesus is the epitome of what it means to be a King and Lord. **We could search for all eternity and still find, there is none like Jesus!** People of the world have come up with many answers to the overwhelming problems that confront society. For some, the answer has been progress, growth, and development. They believe that what's needed to solve the problems is time and the answers will come, for after all, they have the tools of education and man-made governments. For others, the answers have been in the many religions and the development of the self. However, the Scriptures denounce all human viewpoints! **The only solution to the problem of sin and evil in the world is not through any type of improvement or development of the present order. From God's perspective, the solution**

is the rooting up and the over-throwing of the present order. This is what Jesus' second coming will accomplish!

Chapter Nine: The Millennial Reign of Jesus Christ

The millennial reign of Christ carries the awesome blessings of His perfect and righteous rule over all who've placed their trust in Him as Lord and Savior. Revelation 20:1-7 gives six references to the kingdom of Christ as lasting one thousand years. This kingdom is called the millennium, a term that's derived from the Latin words "mille" (one thousand) and "annum" (year). This kingdom will literally fulfill the prayer which Jesus taught His followers to pray in Matthew 6:10. It says, **"Your kingdom come. Your will be done, on earth as it is in heaven."** In other words, the kingdom of Christ is the purpose, plan and glory of God. There are literally hundreds of passages in the Bible that predict an earthly kingdom of God, ruled by God the Son and superseding all the kingdoms of the world. In this study, we'll examine some of these passages holding them out as lines of evidence concerning the kingdom of Christ on earth.

The Kingdom of Christ According to the prophet Daniel

We will examine the words of Daniel 2:31-49. This passage concerns the vision of king Nebuchadnezzar as told by the prophet Daniel. This passage also reveals some things about the future kingdom of Christ, the millennial kingdom. We read, **"Now in the second year of the reign of Nebuchadnezzar, Nebuchadnezzar had dreams; and his spirit was troubled and his sleep left him. Then the king gave orders to call in the magicians, the conjurers, the sorcerers and the Chaldeans to tell the king his dreams. So, they came in and stood before the king.**

The king said to them, 'I had a dream and my spirit is anxious to understand the dream'" (Daniel 2:1-3). The king called the so-called men of wisdom of his kingdom together to interpret his dream, but gave this condition; the wise men first had to tell the king what he had dreamed. The king did not want to leave the interpretation to chance! The king wanted to know whether they'd be able to interpret the dream properly. He wanted a straight and correct interpretation, without deception! In **Daniel 2:10**, we read, **"The Chaldeans answered the king and said, 'There is not a man on earth who could declare the matter for the king, inasmuch as no great king or ruler has ever asked anything like this of any magician, conjurer or Chaldean.'"** In other words, the worldly men of human skill failed, just as the magicians of Pharaoh's court failed (Exodus 8:16-19). This passage shows how impossible it is for humans to interpret dreams from God without the aid of God! Daniel's words to the king confirm the human impossibility. We read, **"Daniel answered before the king and said, 'As for the mystery about which the king has inquired, neither wise men, conjurers, magicians nor diviners are able to declare it to the king'" (Daniel 2:27).** In other words, God was not involved with any of these people! When the men claimed that no one on earth could tell the king what his dream was and then bring the interpretation, the king commanded that all the wise men in the kingdom of Babylon be put to death **(Daniel 2:12).** Daniel and his three friends had not been invited to the dream interpretation meeting, but they were to fall victim to the same command of verse 12. Because of God's sovereignty, Nebuchadnezzar granted them some time. We read, **"So Daniel went in and requested of the king that he would give him time, in order that he might**

declare the interpretation to the king" (Daniel 2:16).
The sovereign God revealed the dream and its
interpretation to Daniel in a night vision **(Daniel 2:19-23)**.
Praise God forevermore! The sovereignty of God, when
rightly understood and embraced, provides much rejoicing
for the Christ follower! In this passage, the sovereignty of
God is on full display!

Daniel said, "**As for you, O king, while on your bed your
thoughts were to what would take place in the future;
and He who reveals mysteries has made known to you
what will take place" (Daniel 2:29)**. Take note that
before bringing the interpretation of the dream, Daniel
made certain to say that this was not his wisdom, but that
God should receive all credit for this interpretation. This is
seen in the phrase, **"He who reveals mysteries."** Daniel
said, **"However, there is a God in heaven who reveals
mysteries, and He has made known to king
Nebuchadnezzar what will take place in the latter days.
This was your dream and the visions in your mind while
on your bed" (Daniel 2:28)**. Notice the phrase **"a God in
heaven who reveals mysteries."** What an awesome
motivation for praying! The prophet Jeremiah, concerning
prayer to God, said these words, **"Call to Me and I will
answer you, and I will tell you great and mighty things
which you do not know" (Jeremiah 33:3)**. Here we see
that Daniel picks up where the wise men left off when they
said, **"there is no one else who could declare it to the
king except the gods" (Daniel 2:11)**. In describing the
king's dream, Daniel issues a direct challenge to the
impotent false religion and gods of Babylon! Since
Babylon is called **"the mother of harlots and of the
abominations of the earth" (Revelation 17:5),** or the
birthplace of all the earth's false religions, Daniel's

declaration of **"a God in heaven"** signals the failure of these false religious systems which sinful men have devised in their futile attempt to fill the empty space that results from the rejection of the one True Living God! There is **"a God in heaven"** and His name is Christ Jesus! And He's still saying, **"I am the way, and the truth, and the life; no one comes to the Father but through Me" (John 14:6).**

Let's examine Daniel's revealing of the dream. This is covered in Daniel 2:31-35. We're told that Nebuchadnezzar's dream was of a statue made of different materials. Then a stone struck the statue's feet and crushed the whole image, which blew away to nothing. The stone, on the other hand, turned into a large mountain. Such a strange dream! The interpretation of the dream follows in Daniel 2:36. Once the king heard that Daniel truly knew the dream, he was convinced that Daniel also had the correct interpretation. Daniel now begins to describe to Nebuchadnezzar what each section of the image represented. In Daniel 2:37, we find the phrase **"king of kings."** The first part of the image was the head of gold. Daniel says that the king is the head of gold, calling him **"king of kings."** While this phrase is a New Testament title of Jesus (1 Timothy 6:15; Revelation 17:14; 19:16), in the Old Testament it's used as a description. Nebuchadnezzar was the king of kings! **His power and rule had conquered many nations, and those who sat on the thrones of these nations served him!** The sovereign God raised up this Gentile king to chasten rebellious Judah and to present His prophetic plan for the ages! As earthly kings go, Nebuchadnezzar was indeed the supreme example of a human king. See Ezekiel 26:7 and Ezra 7:12. In Ezra 7:12, king Artaxerxes of Persia is called a king of kings for the same reason.

The head of gold: **"You are the head of gold" (Daniel 2:38)**. The head of gold is symbolic of Nebuchadnezzar's kingdom, Babylon. Just as the king personified the kingdom, so too did its capital city. Concerning Babylon, Isaiah said, **"Thou shalt take up this proverb against the king of Babylon, and say, 'How hath the oppressor ceased! The golden city ceased'" (Isaiah 14:4), King James Version.** The Historian, Herodotus noted his awe at the sheer amount of gold in Babylon. "It seemed to cover almost everything. Even the walls that encircled the city, noted for such size and width that two chariots could race on them, were plated with gold. The city of Babylon was rightly represented as the head of gold!" God had caused this king to rule. Babylon had conquered the Assyrian Empire, and gained rule over many nations.

Nebuchadnezzar's kingdom stretched south of Jerusalem and east and north to encompass the entire territory covered by the Euphrates and Tigris Rivers! Daniel informed the king that his authority and power came from the Lord God. As a matter of fact, God had spoken through the prophet Ezekiel, **"Thus I will strengthen the arms of the king of Babylon, but the arms of pharaoh will fall. Then they will know that I am the LORD, when I put My sword into the hand of the king of Babylon and he stretches it out against the land of Egypt." (Ezekiel 30:25)** The Babylonian kingdom had been established by God for God's own purposes! Remember the words Daniel had said earlier to Nebuchadnezzar, **"Let the name of God be blessed forever and ever, For wisdom and power belong to Him. It is He who changes the times and the epochs; He removes kings and establishes kings…" (Daniel 2:20-21)** Daniel also said to the king, **"In order that the**

living may know that the Most High is ruler over the realm of mankind…" (Daniel 4:17)

The Breast and Arms of Silver; **(Daniel 2:39)** Daniel prophesied that after the fall of Babylon, a second kingdom would come onto the scene. This kingdom was symbolized in the image by **"its breast and arms of silver" (v 32).** This prophecy was fulfilled when Cyrus, the king of Persia, and Darius, the king of Media, besieged Babylon. This takes place at the end of chapter five. At this point, the world power became the Gentile nation of the Medo-Persian empire. Daniel calls this kingdom **"inferior"** to the Babylonian empire. Daniel is not speaking of the decrease of strength or size.

The Medo-Persian empire was more powerful and larger than Nebuchadnezzar's kingdom, (Daniel 7:5). However, it did not have the unity and structure of government that Babylon had. These truths are seen in the image. Traveling down from head to toe, as the metals decrease in value they increase in strength! The metals go from gold to silver to bronze to iron and then to iron mixed with clay! The decrease in value is the meaning of the term **"inferior."**

The Belly and Thighs of Bronze: (Daniel 2:39). In the dream, the image's **"belly and its thighs of bronze" (v32).** This is the third kingdom. This is the Greek Empire under the leadership of Alexander the Great. Daniel said that this kingdom **"will rule over all the earth."** The Greeks were well known for their bronze armor and weapons. Not only did Alexander crush Darius the Mede's army, but he soon had conquered everyone else as well! Alexander the Great became the ruler of the known world, including Israel, from Europe to Egypt to India!

The Legs of Iron: (Daniel 2:40) The fourth world kingdom that Daniel mentioned was described as one with **"legs of iron" (v33).** Daniel says that kingdom **"crushes and shatters all things" (v 40).** While this kingdom is not named in Daniel, from history we know this to be the Roman Empire. The Roman Empire crushed and destroyed everyone and everything in its path. There was no kingdom in world history that so crushed all its enemies as Rome did. Because iron is much stronger than gold, silver, and bronze, it can crush these metals. In the same manner, Rome crushed and destroyed any opposition to its rule. Dr. Thomas Constable remarks: "Rome defeated the last vestige of the Greek Empire in 31 B.C. and ruled for hundreds of years until A.D. 476 in the Western Roman Empire, and until A.D. 1453 in the Eastern Roman Empire. The eastern and western divisions of this empire (the two legs of iron), crushed all opposition with a brutal strength that surpassed any of its predecessors. Certainly, iron legs fitly symbolized the Roman Empire" (Expository Notes of Dr. Thomas Constable).

Feet Partly of Iron and Partly of Clay: (Daniel 2:41-43) The image progresses down to the **"feet partly of iron and partly of clay" (v33).** Daniel is not describing a fifth kingdom, but an extension of the fourth kingdom. The toes are symbolic of ten divisions in the Roman empire at the time it will be destroyed. In other words, this carries us into a vision that's yet future. The Roman Empire never divided into ten sections; neither did anyone ever conquer it. Rome collapsed from within. The ten toes represent the same kings as the ten horns in Daniel 7:24. The vision tells us that in the future, the Roman Empire will arise once again, with ten kings ruling over it. From these ten kings, the antichrist will arise and subdue three of the kings. This is further explained in the book of Revelation. The devil appears in Revelation 12 as a red dragon having seven heads and ten horns. Then, in chapter 13, the antichrist arises with these same ten horns and seven heads. Jesus Christ will destroy this final Gentile kingdom at His second coming.

The Stone that Crushes: (Daniel 2:44-45). Daniel's imagery is that of **"a stone cut out without hands and it struck the statue on its feet of iron and clay and crushed them" (v 34)**. The imagery used by Daniel is that of a stone crushing the Gentile Kingdoms. The **"stone cut out without hands,"** represents the Lord Jesus Christ, and His second coming to rule over the earth! In the Bible, Jesus has often been referred to as a stone. To the Jewish nation, Jesus is **"the stumbling stone" (Isaiah 8:14; Romans 9:32-33; 1 Peter 2:8)**. To the church, Jesus is **"the corner stone" (Ephesians 2:20; 1 Peter 2:6-7)**. To every Gentile world power, Jesus is **"the stone cut out without hands"** that will bring all Gentile rule to an end! At the second coming of Jesus, He will fulfill the passage that says, **"And Jerusalem will be trampled underfoot by the Gentiles until the times of the Gentiles are fulfilled" (Luke 21:24)**. The times of the Gentiles will continue until the stone strikes the statue! Praise God forevermore!

The phrase **"the times of the Gentiles"** describes the time from Israel's captivity to Babylon to her restoration in the millennial kingdom of God (Revelation 20:1-6). It has been a time which according to God's purpose, Gentiles have controlled, dominated, or threatened Jerusalem. Because of Israel's repeated rebellion before God, God has removed the scepter of power from their kings. The scepter of power was given by God to the Gentile nations, starting with Babylon and its king, Nebuchadnezzar. This is the start of what Jesus called **"the times of the Gentiles."** God is going to bring this era to a close! The revived Roman Empire led by the beast of Revelation 13 (antichrist), will not fall on the stone, the stone will fall on it and crush it! Humanity's greatest effort will inevitably lead to the establishment of the antichrist, and his attempt to rule the world. The best that God will do is the removal of the antichrist and the establishment of His King to rule over the earth! Daniel puts it this way: **"In the days of those kings the God of heaven will set up a kingdom which will never be destroyed, and that kingdom will not be left for another people; it will crush and put an end to all these kingdoms, but it will itself endure forever. Inasmuch as you saw that a stone was cut out of the mountain without hands and that it crushed the iron, the bronze, the clay, the silver and the gold, the great God has made known to the king what will take place in the future; so the dream is true and its interpretation is trustworthy"** (Daniel 2:44-45).

Characteristics of the Millennial Kingdom:

Because the topic of the millennial kingdom is very large and is the subject of many prophecies, our purpose will not be to describe it in detail. Instead, we'll provide a summary of the main characteristics of this 1000-year kingdom of Christ. Let's picture a world ruled and dominated by goodness and righteousness. Let's picture a world where there's no injustice, where no court ever delivers a verdict that's unjust, and where all people are treated fairly. Let's picture a world where racism no longer exists. Let's picture a world where absolute truth marks every area of life, including how people interact with one another. Let's picture a world where the things that are true, right, and noble govern society, business, education and government. Let's picture a world where there's complete, enforced, and permanent peace, where joy prevails and physical health abounds, so much so that people will live for hundreds of years. Picture a world where God has removed the curse from nature, where the environment has been restored to the purity of the Garden of Eden. Picture a world where peace will reign in the animal world, so that **"the wolf will dwell with the lamb, and the leopard will lie down with the young goat, and the calf and the young lion and the fatling together; and a little boy will lead them" (Isaiah 11:6).** Picture a world led and ruled by a perfect and glorious Ruler, who instantly and firmly deals with sin.

Picture a world where nations no longer fight against each other, where disagreements between nations will be judged by the Lord Jesus Christ! Picture a world that provides a high level of social and economic characteristics for the entire earth. Picture a world that will be a time of great prosperity, without poor people or people suffering from lack of economic means. Picture a world which was cursed following Adam's sin, now flourishing and bringing forth abundantly! Picture a world where Satan is bound for the entire thousand years! Picture a world where Satan is cast into the abyss and its door is shut! Picture a world where a seal is placed upon Satan himself making it impossible for him to deceive the nations until a thousand years have elapsed. Picture a world of theocratic rule, where God rules in the Person of Jesus Christ. Picture a world where the rule of Jesus Christ extends both spiritually and literally over the entire earth.

Humanly speaking, the things we have described and pictured may seem other-worldly, far-fetched, and fantasy, one that could never be reality. However, I have good news for you! The things we've been asked to picture describe conditions during the future earthly kingdom of the Lord Jesus Christ!

A Concise Look at The Kingdom of Christ (the millennial kingdom)

      A. **The duration of this kingdom is one thousand years.** Revelation 20:2-7.

      B. **Theocratic Government.** God will rule in the Person of the Lord Jesus Christ, who reigns on the throne of David. Jeremiah 33:15-17; 23:5-6; Ezekiel 37:24-25; Daniel 7:13-14; Luke 1:30-33.

      C. **Representative Government**. The 12 apostles will represent Jesus Christ ruling over the 12 tribes. Church-age and tribulation saints will represent Jesus Christ ruling over the Gentiles. Isaiah 32:1-2; 1 Corinthians 6:2; 2 Timothy 2:12; Luke 22:28-30; Revelation 2:26; 3:21; 5:10; 20:2.

      D. **Universal Government**. Jesus' rule and authority will reach both spiritually and literally over the whole earth. Psalm 2:6-9; 72:8; Daniel 2:35,44; Micah 4:1-2; Zechariah 14:9; Psalm 22:28.

E. **Global Environmental Change**. The heavens and earth will be restored to Garden of Eden-like conditions. This will counter the damage from humanity's long standing abuse as well as the tribulation's catastrophic judgments. Isaiah 64:17; Matthew 19:28.

F. **The populace**. Several different categories of believers will enter the millennial kingdom.

   i. Christ followers raptured at the close of the church age. They return to earth with the Lord at His second coming to enter the kingdom with glorified bodies.

   ii. Believers (Jews and Gentiles) who died before the Church age and tribulation martyrs who will die during the tribulation. This category includes the Old Testament saints as well as those killed during the tribulation for their refusal to worship the Beast. This group will have glorified bodies.

   iii. Believers who survive the tribulation and the sheep and goat judgment. These believers will enter the kingdom in their natural bodies. Ezekiel 37:12-14; Daniel 12:1-2; Isaiah 65:20-25; Matthew 25:31-46; Revelation 20:4-6.

G. **The Curse**. Many aspects of the curse will be reversed. People will live much longer, but dying will still occur. Wild animals will no longer eat and kill one another. Nature will no longer produce earth quakes, hurricanes, typhoons, or volcanic actions. Ezekiel 47:8-12; Isaiah 11:6-9; 65:20-25.

H. **The People of Israel**. The Jewish remnant will finally inhabit and enjoy the Promise Land on a permanent basis. Israel will serve as focal point of all nations. This is because Jesus will reign from Jerusalem. Psalm 105:8-11; Jeremiah 3:15-18; 30:1-3; Ezekiel 37:24-25; 39:25-29; Deuteronomy 30:5.

I. **Universal Peace Prevails**. Implements of war will be destroyed. War will no longer exist between nations. Any disagreements between nations are judged by the Lord from His throne in Jerusalem. Isaiah 2:1-4; 9:6-7; Micah 4:2-3; Zechariah 9:10; Psalm 72:3-7.

J. **Universal Worship**. All the nations will go to Jerusalem to worship the Lord. Isaiah 2:2-4; 56:6-7; Zechariah 8:20-23; 14:16-17; Psalm 22:27; Revelation 15:4; Psalm 86:9.

K. **Worldwide Knowledge of God.** Isaiah 11:9; Psalm 67:2; 72:19; 98:2; Habakkuk 2:14.

L. **Jesus Christ Rules over Israel**. Isaiah 40:10-11; Jeremiah 31:10-11; Micah 5:2.

M. **Jesus Rules over and Judges the Nations**. Isaiah 11:3-5; Revelation 19:15.

N. **The Close of the Millennium**. The 1,000-year reign of the Lord Jesus will close, according to Revelation 20:7-9. It closes with a short-lived rebellion against Jesus as God and King. This rebellion is caused by the loosing of Satan who was bound and incarcerated during the 1,000-year reign. All who take part in this rebellion are deceived by the devil. Those who are deceived have been born during the millennium and were never born again. They reveal their true condition of unbelief as soon as the opportunity presents itself. The rebellion, led by the master deceiver, encompasses the city of Jerusalem in a futile attempt to take it by force. According to Revelation 20:7-9, this doomed rebellion is destroyed by fire which comes from heaven! With the army being destroyed, the devil himself is cast into the lake of fire (Revelation 20:10) where he joins the beast and the false prophet who were thrown into the lake of fire 1,000 years earlier! Their service to Satan resulted in being cast into the lake of fire and brimstone. How sad! The 1,000-year kingdom, the most ideal state imaginable for man apart from the eternal state itself, ends with yet another graphic showing of the depravity and wickedness of the human heart. Even under ideal circumstances, man rebels against God. This should forever close the mouths of those who question the justice of God in judging mankind.

Some Purposes of The Millennial Kingdom

The Bible presents some purposes for the 1,000-year period on earth, with each purpose supporting the need for a literal thousand-year period of time on the earth. Let's examine some of these purposes.

The Rewarding of God's People

There are various promises in the Scripture concerning rewards that are to be presented to the people of God for their faithful service (Isaiah 40:10; Matthew 16:27; 25:34; Colossians 3:24; Revelation 22:12). Christ said, **"come, you who are blessed of My Father, INHERIT THE KINGDOM prepared for you from the foundation of the world" (Matthew 25:34).** In Colossians 3:24, apostle Paul teaches that the Christ follower will receive a just, eternal compensation for his efforts. He uses the phrase, **"the reward of the inheritance."** The millennial kingdom itself is a reward by which the Christ follower will reign with Christ over the earth for 1,000 years (Matthew 19:28; 1 Corinthians 6:2; Revelation 20:4). We must understand and embrace that our responsibilities in the millennial kingdom will be based on our faithfulness in this life. This is reflected in the teaching of Matthew 25:14-30. Remember Jesus' words to the faithful, **"Well done, good**

and faithful servant. You were faithful with a few things, I will put you in charge of many things; enter into the joy of your master" (Matthew 25:21). Randy Alcorn offers these insightful words on this subject: "The idea of service as a reward is foreign to a lot of people who don't like their work, who only put up with their work until it's time to retire. We think that faithful service should be rewarded with a long vacation. But God offers us an opportunity very different from work: More responsibilities is His reward. Increased opportunities are His reward, greater abilities and resources and wisdom and empowerment. We will have sharper minds, stronger bodies, clearer purpose and unabated joy." (Randy Alcorn, Heaven, p. 226). For more study of rewards, examine chapter 13 of this book!

The Fulfillment of Prophecy

Another purpose of the millennial kingdom is the fulfillment of the Old Testament prophecies. In other words, without the millennial kingdom, the Old Testament prophecies are left unfulfilled. I will mention only a few that are yet to be fulfilled.

1. Psalm 72:11 **(All nations and kings will serve Christ)**.

2. Isaiah 9:7 **(Messiah's government must be established on the throne of David)**.

3. Isaiah 60:21 **(Israel will turn to righteousness and inherit the promised land forever)**.

4. Psalm 2:6 **(God's King will be enthroned upon Zion, God's holy mountain)**.

5. Zechariah 9:10 **(All nations must live in peace under Christ's rule)**.

Robert Taylor

Without the millennial kingdom, these as well as many other prophecies would go unfulfilled! God is faithful to His Word. None of these things have taken place yet, so it must take place in the future. The kingdom will be restored to Israel during the millennium. The apostles were looking for it (Acts 1:6), and it will be fulfilled for 1,000 years in the millennial kingdom!

Reemphasizing the Total Depravity of Man

Total depravity is the teaching that fallen man in every area of his being, body, soul, spirit, mind, emotions, etc., is stained by sin. Man, is totally depraved. Because of depravity, nothing good can come from him (Romans 3:10-12), and God must account the righteousness of Jesus Christ to him. This righteousness is received through faith in what Jesus did on the cross. The devil will be bound and incarcerated during the millennial kingdom (Revelation 20:2-3). At the end of the thousand-year kingdom, he'll be loosed, at which time he'll instigate and lead a brief but final rebellion against Jesus Christ, the King (Revelation 20:7-9). We must remember that during the thousand-years on earth, the believers who made it through the tribulation will enter the kingdom in their natural bodies. They will bear children, but God's righteousness is not inherited by these children! The sin nature of these inhabitants will still be a part of them, and some will not submit to Jesus' rule. They will be part of Satan's rebellion against Christ. This rebellion shows that the sin nature of man is man's greatest problem! Man's problem is not his environment. Man's problem is not education. Man's problem is not genetics. Man's problem is that he's totally depraved. Hal Lindsey reminds us, "Spiritual death and all its terrible consequences were inevitably passed on to all the descendants of Adam and Eve. Our first parents' sin caused the whole human race that followed to be born spiritually dead and separated from God. In this condition, cut off from the only One who could guide and empower him to live correctly, man plunged out of control into sin, and its inevitable consequence, suffering and death." (Faith For Earth's Final Hour). Even in an environment such as the millennial kingdom where Jesus Christ is reigning, man will still rebel against the Lord! Even with Christ on the throne in a righteous world, some because of the sin nature will choose to follow Satan's rebellion. How desperate is the need to be reconciled to God through believing in what Jesus did for God and man on the cross?

If you have not called out to God to save you, now would be a good time to do so! The righteousness that God extends is found in the Bible. Paul said the gospel **"is the power of God FOR SALVATION to everyone who believes" (Romans 1:16).** He continues, **"For in it the RIGHTEOUSNESS OF GOD is revealed" (Roman 1:17).** The only solution to man's depravity is the salvation that God gives. In this context, we're told that the **"righteousness of God"** is present in the gospel. **Salvation is this:** God declaring a sinner righteous due to having faith in the person and work of Christ. The moment God declares a person as righteous; He then gives the person His righteousness! The result is, when God looks at you, He sees the righteousness of Christ! It really doesn't get any better than this!

Chapter Ten: A Concise Look at Revelation 20: 1-15

The Millennium (Revelation 20:1-10)

"Then I saw an angel coming from heaven, holding the key of the abyss and a great chain in his hand. And he laid hold of the dragon, the serpent of old, who is the devil and Satan, and bound him for a thousand years" (Revelation 20:1-2).

Because of Jesus' victory on the cross, the devil and his forces are now a defeated bunch! Consequently, during Jesus' kingdom on earth, Satan will be bound and rendered inactive by the sovereign God. The cross of Jesus signaled the ultimate doom of Satan and his evil host of fallen angels (Colossians 2:15). In our passage, we see the angel operating at the command as well as in the sovereign authority of Almighty God. This angel **"laid hold of the dragon."** The phrase **"laid hold of"** means "to be mighty, strong, or master over." This angel operating in the power and authority of God, has the ability needed to seize, hold firmly, and restrain the devil and lock him in this prison with no way of escape! How awesome is that? John is witnessing this angel coming down from heaven with a key and a great chain in his hands. The **"abyss"** is also called the **"bottomless pit" in Revelation 9:1, 2, 11.** The phrase **"bottomless pit"** literally means "shaft of the abyss." This is the place of bondage for fallen angels (demons or unclean spirits). This is the same place called **"the pits of darkness" in 2 Peter 2:4.** Recall from Matthew 8:31 and Luke 8:31 that the demons feared going to this place and begged Christ, during His time on earth, not to send them there! Also, examine the words of Jude 6-7! Take notice of some of the names of Satan. Each name is descriptive of how he operates against God and Christ followers. These names are given as warnings to Christ followers to not take the devil lightly.

"And he threw him into the abyss, and shut it and sealed it over him, so that he would not deceive the nations any longer, until the thousand years were completed; after these things, he must be released for a short time" (Revelation 20:3).

The devil is bound and thrown into the abyss and the door is shut! The key, the chain and the seal point to the power and authority that God has over the devil. These items guarantee that the devil will not be released until God releases him! The devil's release from incarceration will be one thousand years later, **"until the thousand years were completed."** Any temptation to sin during the millennial kingdom will not come from the devil. Notice the phrase **"that he would not deceive the nations."** Satan will not be on earth to bother the believers during the thousand years of Christ's kingdom. Deception is a terrible thing and should be hated by every Christ follower! Deception is defined as "believing a lie for the truth." Jesus called the devil **"a liar and the father of lies" (John 8:44).** The devil lies to lead astray and deceive (2 Thessalonians 2:9-10; Revelation 12:9).

Also, notice that once the devil is bound, he stays bound! He remains bound until the sovereign God looses him. There's an unsound doctrine that has infiltrated the church that says the Christ follower has the power to bind the devil. This teaching is unsound and false! If we're given the power to bind the devil, who keeps letting him loose? Apostle Peter said, **"Be of sober spirit, be on the alert. Your adversary, the devil prowls around like a roaring lion, seeking someone to devour" (1 Peter 5:8).** Peter said the devil is prowling around, not bound! We do not have the power or the authority to bind the devil! Only God does! As Christ followers, we can **"resist him, firm in our faith" (1 Peter 5:9).** The prophecy of these three verses reveals this angel is empowered for six functions. They are as follows:

1. **Lay hold on the dragon.**

2. **Bind him for 1000 years.**

3. **Cast him into the abyss.**

4. **Shut him up**.

5. **Set a seal on him which renders him inactive in his work of deceiving.**

6. **Loose him after the 1000 years**.

God has not empowered nor authorized the Christ follower to do any of these six things! At the end of 1000 years, Satan will be released from his incarceration to do what he does best, to deceive the nations. He will find many unsaved descendants of those who entered the kingdom. There will be a very large number that will follow the devil to their destruction. The number as we're told in Revelation 20:8 is **"like the sand of the seashore."** That's a lot of people!

"Then I saw thrones, and they sat on them, and judgment was given to them. And I saw the souls of those who had been beheaded because of their testimony of Jesus and because of the word of God, and those who had not worshiped the beast or his image, and had not received the mark on their forehead and on their hand; and they came to life and reigned with Christ for a thousand years" (Revelation 20:4).

We now arrive at a passage that deals with the populace of the millennial kingdom. We've covered these groups of people under the section entitled, **"A Concise Look at the Kingdom of Christ (the millennial kingdom) section F (chapter 9)."** I will note that those believers who enter the millennial kingdom will during that period beget children. These children will also, regardless of the glorious and personal presence of King Jesus, need to receive Christ as their Lord and Savior. **This fact provides the potential for another group of people in the kingdom; unbelievers with natural bodies and sin natures. This group of people will be susceptible to the deceptions of the devil when he's loosed from the abyss.**

In our passage, John makes mention of those who are described as **"beheaded because of their testimony of Jesus and because of the word of God."** This is a detailed description that fits only one group of people. These are the tribulation saints who for refusing to worship the beast are put to death. The context of this experience can be found in Revelation 6:9-11; 13:15-17. The group is shown to be in heaven in Revelation 7:9-17. John declares this group of saints **"came to life and reigned with Christ for a thousand years."** The phrase **"came to life"** indicates that these saints are resurrected and live again.

132

Thank God for Jesus being the resurrection and the life!
All who die believing in the Lord Jesus, will live again with
Him forevermore. How great is that? Jesus said it best with
these words, **"I am the resurrection and the life; he who
believes in Me will live even if he dies" (John 11:25).**
Jesus is the One who can cause the dead to come to life!
No resurrection exists outside of Christ Jesus!

**"The rest of the dead did not come to life until the
thousand years were completed. This is the first
resurrection. Blessed and holy is the one who has a part
in the first resurrection; over these the second death has
no power, but they will be priests of God and of Christ
and will reign with Him for a thousand years"
(Revelation 20:5-6).**

Who are **"the rest of the dead"** in verse five? This refers
to all unbelieving dead of all time, beginning with Cain
through the end of the tribulation. The only exceptions are
the beast and the false prophet. **"These two were thrown
alive into the lake of fire which burns with brimstone"
(Revelation 19:20).** There is no resurrection for the beast
and the false prophet, because they were already thrown
alive into the lake of fire which burns with brimstone! Let's
examine the phrase **"the first resurrection."** It is the
resurrection found in the words, **"and they came to life"
(Revelation 20:4).** It has three primary phases. They are:

1. **The resurrection of Jesus as the first fruits** (1
   Corinthians 15:23; Revelation 1:5).

2. **The resurrection of the church** (the dead in
   Christ, 1 Corinthians 15:23; 1 Thessalonians 4:16).

3. **The resurrection of Old Testament saints and tribulation martyrs** (Revelation 20:4; Isaiah 26:19; Daniel 12:1-3).

We're told that the **"rest of the dead"** (unbelievers), will be resurrected in the second resurrection, described in Revelation 20:12-13. John says, **"blessed and holy is the one who has a part in the first resurrection."** Believers are the recipients of God's salvation which points to being blessed! All believers will share in the wonderful blessings of the millennial kingdom and the eternal state. Those who take part in the first resurrection are blessed because of being delivered from the power of the second death! John says **"over these the second death has no power."** Wow! How awesome is that statement? Let's examine it.

The term **"second death"** speaks of being eternally consigned to the lake of fire that follows the resurrection of all the unsaved. It speaks of being separated from God for all eternity. Remember, death means to be separated! John says, **"This is the second death, the lake of fire" (Revelation 20:14).** The second death comes to those having no part in the first resurrection. In other words, the second death comes from having only **one birth!** Therefore, Jesus told Nicodemus, **"Truly, truly, I say to you, unless one is born again he cannot see the kingdom of God" (John 3:3).** Having only **one birth** will not get you into the kingdom of God! Man, is born (physical birth) spiritually dead. Because of this, man needs a **second birth** (spiritual birth) by exercising faith in Jesus Christ. If a person experiences only **one birth**, then because of being spiritually dead, the person must experience **two deaths** (physical and the second death). However, if the person has **two births** (physical and spiritual) he may experience physical death before the rapture of the church, but this person **can never face the second death because of the first resurrection!** The second death can have no power over the believer because of Christ Jesus (Hebrews 2:14; 1 Corinthians 15:54).

"When the thousand years are completed, Satan will be released from his prison, and will come out to deceive the nations which are in the four corners of the earth, Gog and Magog, to gather them together for the war; the number of them is like the sand of the seashore. And they came up on the broad plain of the earth and surrounded the camp of the saints and the beloved city, and fire came down from heaven and devoured them. And the devil who deceived them was thrown into the lake of fire and brimstone, where the beast and the false prophet are also; and they will be tormented day and night forever and ever" (Revelation 20:7-10).

We arrive at the climax of the millennial kingdom as shown in this passage. On being released from his incarceration, Satan wastes no time in getting back to what he does best. He, once again, engages in his schemes of deceiving, disruption, and warfare. Those who are targeted for temptation and deception are the descendants of those who entered the kingdom in their natural bodies. William Hoste in his book, The Visions of John the Divine, pp. 160-61; comments: "The golden age of the kingdom will last a thousand years, during which righteousness will reign, and peace, prosperity, and the knowledge of God be universally enjoyed. But this will not entail universal conversion, and all profession must be tested...Will not a thousand years under the beneficent sway of Christ and the manifested glory of God suffice to render men immune to his (Satan's) temptations, will they not have radically changed for the better, and become by the altered conditions of life and the absence of satanic temptations, children of God and lovers of His will? Alas! **It will be proved once more that man whatever his advantages and environment, apart from the grace of God and the new birth, remains at heart only evil and at enmity with God."** Robert Govett, in his book, The Apocalypse Expounded, pp. 506-8; suggests four reasons why Satan must be loosed after a thousand years: "1. To demonstrate that man even under the most favorable circumstances will fall into sin if left to his own choice. 2. To demonstrate the foreknowledge of God who foretells the acts of men as well as His own acts. 3. To demonstrate the incurable wickedness of Satan. 4. To justify eternal punishment, that is, to show the unchanged character of wicked people even under divine jurisdiction for a long period of time."

In our passage, the term **"Gog and Magog"** is used with no explanation. It's used to designate the nations from **"the four corners of the earth."** In other words, this invasion force comes from all over the world. This term, as used in Ezekiel 38, is descriptive of a rebellious and war-like people and for nations that are in rebellion against God and His people. They are destroyed by fire from heaven. Their judgment is decisive and instantaneous. The nations that rebel against God are many and are described as **"the sand of the seashore."** This last rebellion against God results in a gigantic disaster on the part of **"Gog and Magog."** Examine Psalm 2:1-9 which predicts this end time rebellion. This signals the end of the road for the nations who rebel against the Christ. This signals the end of the road for Satan as he joins his partners in crime (the beast and false prophet) who've been in the lake of fire for a thousand years. This passage teaches that both the beast and the false prophet are still in the lake of fire and brimstone. They've been experiencing torment for a thousand years and will continue to be tormented **"day and night forever and ever."** The lake of fire and brimstone prepared for the devil and his angels is also the destination of all who follow Satan! **In eternity, there are two possible destinations: heaven or hell. There's no such place called purgatory. Purgatory, according to Catholic Church doctrine, is an intermediate state after physical death in which those destined for heaven "undergo purification so as to achieve the holiness necessary to enter the joy of heaven." The doctrine of purgatory is false! You are headed for one of two destinations. If you want heaven, call out to Christ Jesus to save you. After all, the other destination was not prepared for you, but for the devil and his angels!** This ends our discussion of the millennial kingdom of Christ Jesus.

The Great White Throne Judgment (Revelation 20:11-15)

"Then I saw a great white throne and Him who sat upon it, from whose presence earth and heaven fled away, and no place was found for them" (Revelation 20:11).

This is the final judgment of history. It follows the close of the millennial kingdom. This is judgment day! John sees the Judge who is seated on His throne of judgment and all the accused standing before Him. The unsaved will be forever removed by God. This judgment prepares the way for the making of the new heavens and earth which have never nor will ever be touched by sin! The throne is **"great"** because of the majesty of God and the significance of the business to be transpired. The throne is **"white"** because it symbolizes the holiness and righteousness of God. The holiness and righteousness of God is the standard by which the unsaved are judged for their sins. The Bible teaches that man needs the righteousness of God to avoid this judgment. The verdicts and the penalty of the verdicts are righteous and just. In Romans 2:5-6, apostle Paul speaks of this judgment. Paul says**, "But because of your stubbornness and unrepentant heart you are storing up wrath for yourself in the day of wrath and revelation of the righteous judgment of God, who will render to each person according to his deeds."** This judgment is followed by the creation of the new heavens and earth and the eternal state of the redeemed. Let's examine the phrase **"earth and heaven fled away."**

The use for the earth as we know it is over. The earth now has been reshaped by the devastating tribulation judgments, restored during the millennium, and now God creates a new heaven and a new earth where only righteousness dwells! It will never be touched by sin! Apostle Peter tells us; **"Looking for and hastening the coming of the day of God, because of which the heavens will be destroyed by burning, and the elements will melt with intense heat! But according to His promise we are looking for a new heavens and a new earth, in which righteousness dwells" (2 Peter 3:12-13).** In other words, the new heavens and the new earth are this way because righteousness has settled in and taken up permanent residence!

"And I saw the dead, the great and the small, standing before the throne, and books were opened; and another book was opened, which is the book of life; and the dead were judged from the things which were written in the books, according to their deeds. And the sea gave up the dead which were in it, and death and Hades gave up the dead which were in them; and they were judged, every one of them according to their deeds" (Revelation 20:12-13).

The people who are judged are **"the great and the small."** This is in reference to the fact none of this group are exempt. This is because they had no part in the first resurrection (Revelation 20:5-6). All who die without Jesus Christ, regardless of their position in life must stand before this throne. This excludes the beast and the false prophet who already have been cast into the lake of fire and brimstone. **The source of their resurrection is described as follows: the sea, death, and Hades. In other words, it refers to those who died at sea and were not buried in the ground (sea) those who were buried in the ground, cremated, or destroyed in any other way on earth (death) and the place which houses their souls (Hades). The sea and death contains their bodies, while Hades contains their souls.** Their judgment is made based on the books which were opened. The book of life refers to those who are saved and have eternal life. The other books contain the records of their deeds. God has kept perfect, comprehensive, and detailed records of every person's life, and those deeds are measured against God's perfect, holy, and righteous standard! I thank God for Jesus and the salvation He's given me. There's no way I could stand before this judgment without Him!

"Then death and Hades were thrown into the lake of fire. This is the second death, the lake of fire. And if anyone's name was not found written in the book of life, he was thrown into the lake of fire" (Revelation 20:14-15).

The second death is eternal separation and torment in the lake of fire. Only the unsaved will experience this place. An eternal separation is made between all who have eternal life and all who have eternal death. **"Then death and Hades were thrown into the lake of fire."** This phrase is not about these places being destroyed in the lake of fire. It simply means the inhabitants of these places. Please hear this! Those who die in their sins will die a second death in eternity. They will be judged and sentenced to the lake that burns with fire and brimstone. If you are not saved, please call out to Jesus to save you and He will!

Chapter Eleven: Eternity... The Eternal State (new heaven and new earth)

Revelation 21-22 brings before us the wonderful picture of eternity which follows the 1,000-year kingdom reign of Christ. In Revelation 21:1-8, we're given the main features of this period. The old heaven and earth has been **"destroyed by burning" (2 Peter 3:10-12)**, and a new heaven and earth created in which circumstances are thoroughly and completely different than in the present earth. Apostle Peter calls this a "new heavens and a new earth, **in which righteousness dwells" (2 Peter 3:13).** The circumstances of the new heavens and earth are thoroughly and completely different because righteousness has settled in and taken up exclusive residence! Eternity is seen as the place where God will dwell with His people. God will be in fellowship with His people and present in the world where sorrow is excluded and unbelief is no more. Imagine a time where every follower of Christ will be able to experience without hindrance God's awesome blessings of redemption! Praise God forevermore!

The Holy City...New Jerusalem

The primary feature of the new heaven and the new earth is seen in the words, **"coming down out of heaven from God" (Revelation 21:2).** Concerning the holy city, details are given starting in Revelation 21:9. There are differing opinions as to whether the new Jerusalem is in reference to the millennial period or the eternal state. After careful consideration, the description of the holy city is that of the city as it is in the eternal state, after the millennial period has ended. Walvoord says, "It is not impossible, however, that the heavenly Jerusalem was in existence before this period, as it is not said to be created at this time. The new heavens and new earth are said to be created, but the new Jerusalem comes down from heaven. Some believe, therefore, that the heavenly Jerusalem will be a satellite city throughout the millennial reign of Christ and in this city resurrected and translated saints will dwell. By contrast, those in their natural bodies will live on the millennial earth itself. While there is no clear Scripture which supports this concept and it must be held merely as an inference; it would solve a number of problems incident to the relationship of resurrected and translated beings to those still in their natural bodies who will conduct themselves in a normal way on the earth. Undoubtedly if this is the case, those in the heavenly Jerusalem will be able to commute to the millennial earth throughout the thousand-year reign of Christ and participate in its activities."

Revelation 21:1 "Then I saw a new heaven and a new earth; for the first heaven and the first earth passed away, and there is no longer any sea."

Let me remind the reader that in Revelation chapter twenty, John was shown an ideal time on earth when the devil was bound and King Jesus and the saints ruled for one thousand years. As awesome and wonderful as the kingdom of Christ will be with many of the promises of God concerning Israel, the earthly Jerusalem, and the renovated earth coming into fulfillment, it is not the ultimate plan of God!

After the millennial kingdom and Satan's brief but final rebellion, the apostle John witnessed the original earth and heaven flee away. John said, **"Then I saw a great white throne and Him who sat upon it, from whose presence earth and heaven fled away, and no place was found for them" (Revelation 20:11).** In the process (Revelation

20:12-13), the earth and sea gave up the dead who stood before God for judgment. During the millennial kingdom, sin and death had not yet been eliminated (Isaiah 65:20; Revelation 20:9). Now apostle John sees the creation of a new heaven and earth which differs remarkably from the old order. In other words, the new creation is perfect! There's no more sin or death which results from sin. All who populate the new earth enjoy full, unveiled communion with God!

The Old Testament prophets, when prophesying about end time events, saw glimpses of the eternal state. The Spirit of God revealed through these men that there would be a new heavens and a new earth (Isaiah 65:17; 66:22) and that death would be removed (Isaiah 25:8; Hosea 13:14). However, their visions of the eternal state were many times intertwined with revelation pertaining to the millennial kingdom making it hard to draw a clear distinction between the two (Isaiah 65:17-20). In Isaiah 65:17, Isaiah mentions, **"the new heavens and a new earth: (the eternal state)"**, and in 65:20, Isaiah mentions death and dying, **"the youth will die at the age of one hundred" (the millennial kingdom).** In our passage of Revelation 21:1, John is shown aspects of the eternal state that are markedly different from those of the millennial kingdom. In other words, starting with the Revelation 21:1, we're no longer in the millennial kingdom: **there's no more sin, death, sea, or Temple.**

Then I Saw a New Heaven and a New Earth

The conjunction **"then"** connects what follows with the previous chapter. In other words, the creation of a new heaven and a new earth is in response to the uprooting and removal of the previous heaven and earth which fled away and gave up the dead (Revelation 20:11). Recall, as

Revelation chapter 21 begins in the chronology of end times, all the enemies of God from all ages, fallen angels and men, including the devil, the beast, the false prophet is now in the eternal lake of fire and brimstone. They are out of God's presence forever. They are gone from the presence of God, His saints and holy angels forever! Also, the entire universe as we know it has been destroyed. Now that all the ungodly are gone, God creates a new heaven and earth that will be the eternal dwelling place of the redeemed! How awesome is that? It gets even better! The word *new* is in the sense that what is old has become useless and obsolete, and should be replaced by what is new. In all such cases, the new is superior in kind to the old. The quality of new heaven and new earth is totally different from the one we presently know. It's no wonder that we won't even have any remembrance of the one that now exists.

The restorative work prior to the millennial kingdom was a regeneration (Matthew 19:28), not a completely new created order as John says to us. Jesus said to His disciples, **"Truly I say to you, that you who have followed Me, in the regeneration when the Son of Man will sit on His glorious throne, you also shall sit upon twelve thrones, judging the twelve tribes of Israel" (Matthew 19:29).** Jesus is speaking about the restorative work prior to the millennial kingdom. This is demonstrated by the fact that after the millennial kingdom, the earth and sea still contained all the unsaved dead of history. Though the millennial earth was restored in order to recover from the devastating tribulation judgments, sin and death remained on the earth. In the new heavens and new earth, sin and death are totally purged from the created order. God revealed to the Old Testament prophets that the first heavens and earth would be done away with (Psalm

102:25-26; Isaiah 51:6) and be replaced by a new heavens and earth (Isaiah 65:17-20).

As earlier mentioned, the visions of the Old Testament prophets often intermingled aspects from both the millennial kingdom and the eternal state, the differences sometimes being presented out of their chronological sequence. For example, Isaiah saw the new heavens and earth, but continued on to describe a blessed time which included sin and death. Sin and death are not compatible with the eternal state, but are compatible with the millennial kingdom. Every serious student of Bible prophecy is aware that there are many instances of prophecies given out of their chronological sequence. This should not surprise us or cause us to misinterpret Bible passages.

Many Christ followers have asked me, "when we get to heaven, will we remember what happened down here?" Isaiah helps with the answer. He said, **"For behold, I create a new heavens and a new earth; And the former things will not be remembered or come to mind" (Isaiah 65:17).** Notice the phrase, **"And the former things will not be remembered or come to mind."** The answer to the question of remembering things from earth while in heaven is **NO, WE WILL NOT!** If there was a remembrance of the former things, we'd remember things that are contaminated with sin! That's just not possible in the eternal state, of which Isaiah speaks of in verse 17. Praise God forevermore!

According to John, there's coming a new heaven and a new earth. What the prophet Isaiah predicted is now a reality in this vision of apostle John. The earth in which we live is temporary and disposable. We can't improve upon it, we can't preserve it. The whole idea of trying to preserve the earth comes from the human viewpoint and is contrary to the will and plan of God. There's a law of thermodynamics called the law of entropy. This law states that matter is continually breaking down and tending toward disorder. Because the law of entropy is subject to the sovereignty of God, the earth in which we live is breaking down. God doesn't intend for this present earth to remain! He's going to replace this earth with a new heaven and a new earth.

The First Heaven and the First Earth Passed Away

Apostle Peter sheds some insight about this phrase. **Peter said, "But the day of the Lord will come like a thief, in which the heavens will pass away with a roar and the elements will be destroyed with intense heat, and the earth and its works will be burned up. Since all these things are to be destroyed in this way, what sort of people ought you to be in holy conduct and godliness, looking for and hastening the coming of the day of God, because of which the heavens will be destroyed by burning, and the elements will melt with intense heat! But according to His promise we are looking for new heavens and a new earth, in which righteousness dwell"(2 Peter 3:10-13).** The phrase, **"day of the Lord"** in this context, is in reference to the specific interventions of God in human history for judgment. Here, Peter uses this phrase for the time after the millennial kingdom and before the creation of the new heavens and new earth. We know that Peter is speaking of the eternal state because of the phrase, **"in which righteousness dwells."** The entire universe is new because righteousness is now settled in and has taken up permanent residence. With the passing away of the first heaven and the first earth, we're shown the fulfillment of the Lord's prophecies about the permanence of the Word of God. In Luke 21:33, our Lord said, **"Heaven and earth will pass away, but My words will**

not pass away." In other words, the purpose of the Lord, which is set forth by His written Word, reaches not just beyond our present life, but beyond this whole created order. God's Words are surer than the physical world around us. The temporary nature of this present world is to serve as a great motivation for Christ followers to invest in heavenly realities!

No More Sea

The fact that there's no sea in the eternal state provides a helpful aid when interpreting the many passages in the Old Testament. In passages that describe times of tremendous blessing, if the "sea" is mentioned, then we understand the passage can't be related to the eternal state, but is describing conditions of the millennial kingdom. The fact that there's no more sea means that the eternal state is vastly different from the present earth. It's vastly different because 75 percent of this earth is covered with water. Water plays a vital role in the lives of people and plant life. The amount of water in a human body averages between 50-75 percent. Plants as well as animals are mostly water. There's water in the oceans, there's water under the ground, and there's water in the skies. There's water everywhere! Our existence is water-based. Severe dehydration caused by lack of water will kill us. John is telling us the new heavens and earth is not dependent on water any more. Also, whatever changes that accompany glorified bodies will not depend on the consumption of water to exist.

We live and are dependent on a water-based environment. There's water everywhere! The phrase **"There is no longer any sea"** verifies the significant difference of the new heaven and a new earth. Seeing that the new heaven and the new earth have no sea indicates that in our glorified state, no water will be needed.

Revelation 21:2 "And I saw the holy city, new Jerusalem, coming down out of heaven from God, made ready as a bride for her husband."

In Revelation 3:12, Jesus refers to the new Jerusalem as **"the city of My God"** and promised those who overcome that He'd write upon him the name of the city. In biblical times, names often spoke of a person's character. Having the Lord write His name on us speaks of us being identified with Him! How awesome is that? Having the Lord write His name on us as belonging to Him! It just doesn't get any better than this! The holy city, new Jerusalem, is the final destination of all the redeemed of the Lord. Hebrews 13:14 says, **"For here we do not have a lasting city, but we are seeking the city which is to come."** This passage is referring to **"the holy city, new Jerusalem, coming down out of heaven from God."** As Christ followers, we have no continuing city on earth, but seek the one to come. Hebrews 11:10 shares with us, **"For he was looking for the city which has foundations, whose architect and builder is God."** A part of living by faith means that we, like Abraham are looking for the new Jerusalem, a city whose architect is God. Apostle Paul when teaching on the New Covenant compared the present earthly Jerusalem with **"the Jerusalem above"** (Galatians 4:24-26). Hebrews 12:22-24 reads, **"But you have come to Mount Zion and to the city of the living God, the heavenly Jerusalem, and to myriads of angels, to the general assembly and church of the firstborn who are enrolled in heaven, and to God, the Judge of all, and to the spirits of the righteous made perfect, and to Jesus, the mediator of a new covenant, and to the sprinkled blood, which speaks better than the blood of Abel."**

Once again, we see that the new Jerusalem is a literal city which God has prepared as the dwelling place for all believers in their glorified existence after this life (John 14:2-3). Who are the inhabitants of this city? We have myriads of angels, the church of the firstborn, and the spirits of the righteous made perfect (the Old Testament. Saints in distinction from the church). In this passage, Mount Zion is not the earthly one in Jerusalem, but God's heavenly abode. The terms Mount Zion, city of the living God, the heavenly Jerusalem are synonymous for heaven itself. The Bible shares about Abraham, Isaac and Jacob, **"But as it is, they desire a better country, that is, a heavenly one. Therefore God is not ashamed to be called their God; for He has prepared a city for them"** **(Hebrews 11:16).** This city has always been in existence. Abraham, Isaac and Jacob looked for that city and one day went there! All of the saints that have departed this life are gone there! In one of his teachings, John MacArthur states, "I believe Jesus left the earth, went back to the heavenly Jerusalem, the city who has…that has a foundation whose builder and maker is God…He went back to the heavenly Jerusalem where there are just men whose spirits are there and the angels are there and God is there and, of course, Christ is there, and He went back there to prepare a place for us. And some day He's going to bring us to that place. It's important then to see that the new Jerusalem exists even now in some form, it's really heaven; it's where God is. And when a believer dies, they go to the place the Lord has for them. But someday when God creates a whole new infinite universe, that heaven, that third heaven, that Father's house, that new Jerusalem, that city whose builder and maker is God is going to come down and descend into the midst of the new universe. All the glorified of all the ages will live in that city because they'll all live in the Father's house where Jesus is gone. And if He's gone now…listen carefully…if He's gone there now to prepare a place now, it's being prepared in a place that now exists. And the new heaven and the new earth don't now exist." (The New Heaven and the New Earth, Part 1).

"Made Ready as a Bride Adorned for her Husband."

Many read this and say this is about the church. How, we've already seen that the new Jerusalem is the home of all the redeemed, and not just the church.

Revelation 21:3-4 "And I heard a loud voice from the throne, saying, "Behold, the tabernacle of God is among men, and He will dwell among them, and they shall be His people, and God Himself will be among them. And He will wipe away every tear from their eyes; and there will no longer be any death; there will no longer be any mourning, or crying, or pain; the first things have passed away."

Every Christ follower has the presence of the indwelling Spirit of God. This presence affords us the possibility of fellowship and intimacy with God. Apostle Paul tells us, "Or do you not know that your body is a temple of the Holy spirit who is in you, whom you have from God, and that you are not your own?" (1 Corinthians 6:19). In the church age this is a tremendous blessing for every Christ follower! This passage is about the spiritual union of Christ followers with Christ and speaks of intimate communion. However intimate this is, it's still veiled. We still have the sin nature that at times hinder our intimacy with God. As long as we remain in these natural bodies, an unveiled view of God is not possible. No living soul has ever seen God in the fullness of His glory. God is invisible and He **"dwells in unapproachable light" (1 Timothy 6:16).** The Psalmist had this to say about God, **"You are clothed with**

splendor and majesty, covering Yourself with light as with a cloak" (Psalm 104:1-2). In other words, in our natural bodies, exposure to God would mean instant death. But in our passage (Revelation 21:3), we're told that **"the tabernacle of God is among men, and He will dwell among them."** How awesome is this? Our fellowship with God will be UNHINDERED! Because of being in eternity, in our glorified, resurrected bodies, the unapproachable light in which God dwells is now very approachable! Praise God forevermore!

Of all the wonderful blessings that come with the eternal state, God dwelling with us is emphasized first! For the Christ follower, I believe that God being among men, and dwelling among men is the absolute greatest in the Bible! God being and dwelling among men has been the great purpose of our Kinsman-Redeemer, the Lord Jesus Christ. Since the first Adam rebelled and was kicked out of the Garden of Eden (as well as being removed from God's presence), every correspondence between God and man has been with this goal in mind; God dwelling among men. In the eternal state, God dwells with us in all His fullness, all His glory. There's no longer a Holy of Holies in a temple or tabernacle, there's no longer a pillar of cloud by day or a pillar of fire by night! God comes and dwells with us. God comes and makes His home with us, and this is the awesome reality of heaven. This is the awesome reality of the eternal state! Our Lord Jesus said it best with these words, **"Blessed are the pure in heart, for they shall see God" (Matthew 5:8).** Now, through faith, we see God, but in the eternal state, we see God face to face.

Jesus as the last Adam (1 Corinthians 15:45) and our Kinsman-Redeemer has restored the full, unveiled fellowship between God and man, to the way it was between God and the first Adam. This is a tremendous blessing of eternity with Jesus Christ! I'm reminded of the title to a song written by the Jackson Five entitled **"Got To Be There."** In reference to the holy city, new Jerusalem, coming down out of heaven from God, I got to be there! How about you? You can be there if you'll believe what Jesus did on the cross was for you.

In the eternal state, sin is no more. Alleluia! This is descriptive of the perfect conditions of the new Jerusalem. When sin entered the realm of man, the door for death, pain, and suffering was also opened. The pain, suffering, sorrow, misery, and death all come because of sin. In the eternal state to come, after the millennial kingdom, sin will be no more. All the saints will be glorified with a nature confirmed in righteousness. **The saints will be "Able not to sin and not able to sin."** How awesome is that? The reason there's no longer any death is the absence of sin. This is the fulfillment of prophecy spoken of by many of the Old Testament prophets. Speaking of God, Isaiah said, "He will swallow up death for all time, and the Lord God will wipe tears away from all faces" (Isaiah 25:8). We must remember that death was not part of the original created order. Death came by the sin of Adam (Genesis 3:19; Romans 5:12). Sin and death are destroyed in the uprooting and removal of this present order (Revelation 20:14). John goes on to say, "the first things have passed away."

These first things departed when the first heaven and earth passed away (Revelation 21:1). Apostle Paul encourages the Christ follower to maintain a heavenly or eternal point of view in their day to day lives. We are to look past what is temporary, what is perishing and look to that which is eternal. Paul said, "For momentary, light affliction is producing for us an eternal weight of glory far beyond all comparison. While we look not at the things which are seen, but at the things which are not seen; for the things, which are seen are temporal, **but the things which are not seen are ETERNAL"** (2 Corinthians 4:17-18).

Revelation 21:5-7 "And He who sits on the throne said, "Behold, I am making all things new." And He said, "Write, for these words are faithful and true." Then He said to me, "It is done. I am the Alpha and the Omega, the beginning and the end. I will give to the one who thirsts from the spring of the water of life without cost. He who overcomes will inherit these things, and I will be his God and he will be My son."

The One who sits on the throne is God the Father. He is the One who John saw in Revelation 4:1-11 and Revelation 5:1-14. The word **"behold"** means to look upon with awe and amazement. God is making all things new in kind or quality. In other words, it's better! This passage speaks of the fact that the new heaven and new earth will far exceed anything which we could ever have imagined! It just doesn't get any better than this! John is telling us about the wonders of heaven, the eternal state. The present creation which continues to groan under corruption does not fit the new heaven and new earth. In our passage, the present creation has been delivered from corruption by God making all things new. Paul tells us, **"For the anxious longing of the creation waits eagerly for the revealing of the sons of God. For the creation was subjected to futility, not willingly, but because of Him who subjected it IN HOPE that the creation itself also will be set free from its slavery to corruption into the freedom of the glory of the children of God. For we know that the whole creation groans and suffers the pains of childbirth together until now. And not only this, but also, we ourselves groan within ourselves, waiting eagerly for**

**our adoption as sons, the redemption of our body"
(Romans 8:19-23).**

We must understand and embrace the truth that the redemption spoken of in the book of Revelation is much wider than the individual redemption of sinful man. It reaches out to the redemption of the new heaven and new earth. While the Christ follower looks forward to the glorified body (redemption of our body), creation also has a hope! The hope of creation is to 'be set free from its slavery to corruption." This hope is realized in the eternal state. God's words are faithful and true! The things that we've read may seem beyond belief for many that are living under the oppressive control of death and dying, but you can take God at His word! The Bible shares, **"God is not a man, that He should lie, nor a son of man, that He should repent; Has He said, and will He not do it? Or has He spoken, and will He not make it good?" (Numbers 23:19).** The phrase **"faithful and true"** remind us of Christ Jesus. When Christ rode forth at His second coming, He was called **"Faithful and True"** (Revelation 19:11) and **"The Word of God"** (Revelation 19:13). This should not surprise us since the Father and the Son are one God.

The "water of life" is said to be without cost. In other words, the water of life is a gift, given without payment, given undeservedly. It is redemption! It's given to those who are thirsty. It reminds me of the wells of salvation which the prophet Isaiah spoke about (Isaiah 12:3). It reminds me of the conversation that Jesus had with the woman at the well. The account is found in John 4:10-14. Jesus said to her, **"But whoever drinks of the water that I will give him shall never thirst; but the water that I will give him will become in him a well of water springing up to eternal life" (John 4:14).** The only condition of receiving the water of life is to thirst! The powerful result of Jesus' work on the cross is that eternal life, which is infinitely costly, is now available for the asking! Are you thirsty for eternal life? Have you a longing in your soul that nothing seems to meet? Call on Jesus to save you. Call on Jesus for the water of life!

To the overcomer, God says, **"I will be his God and he will be My son."** What an awesome privilege this is! Those who receive Jesus as Lord, receive the right to claim the exalted title of "children of God!" The term "son of God" is about all who are of direct descent from God. We know that angels were created directly by God and are called "sons of God" (Genesis 6:2, 4; Job 1:6; 2:1; 38:7). We know that Adam was created directly by God and is called the "son of God" (Luke 3:38). We know that the Christ follower, born of the Spirit of God, are the "sons of God" (John 1:12-13). Being born again, the overcomer has the Spirit of adoption, who recognizes him as a son and therefore an heir. Apostle Paul said it best with these words, **"For all who are being led by the Spirit of God, these are sons of God. For you have not received a spirit of slavery leading to fear again, but you have received a spirit of adoption as sons by which we cry out, 'Abba! Father!'" The Spirit Himself testifies with our spirit that we are children of God, and if children, heirs also, heirs of God and fellow heirs of Christ, if indeed we suffer with Him so that we may also be glorified with Him (Romans 8: 14-17). Also, "Blessed be the God and Father of our Lord Jesus Christ, who has blessed us with every spiritual blessing in the heavenly places in Christ, just as He chose us in Him before the foundation of the world, that we would be holy and blameless before Him in love. He predestined us to adoption as sons through Jesus Christ to Himself, according to the kind intention of His will" (Ephesians**

1:3-5). These are awesome descriptions of the relationship between that of the overcomer and God. To the overcomer, God says, **"I will be his God and he will be My son."**

Revelation 21:9-11 "Then one of seven angels who had the seven bowls full of the seven last plagues came and spoke with me, saying, "Come here, I will show you the bride, the wife of the Lamb. And he carried me away in the Spirit to a great and high mountain, and showed me the holy city, Jerusalem, coming down out of heaven from God, having the glory of God. Her brilliance was like a very costly stone, as a stone of crystal clear jasper."

The holy city coming down out of heaven from God is called **"the bride, the wife of the Lamb"** because the character of the city is drawn from its occupants. The occupants of the city, now enlarged beyond just the church, are the redeemed from every age. This is the eternal bride of Christ. Because the people of the city are eternally connected to Christ, the Lamb, it's seen as a bride. Because the people of the city are eternally faithful to Christ, the Lamb, it's seen as a bride. Concerning the city, John says **"having the glory of God."** The city has the glory of God in it! This city bears the total expression of the glory of God. How awesome is that? The city brings forth the unlimited, unveiled glory of God. This is the Shekinah, the visible manifestation of the presence of God. Whenever God manifests His invisible attributes, He manifests them as light! The Scripture in this regard is very clear. Paul said of God, **"He who is the blessed and only Sovereign, the King of kings and Lord of Lords, who alone possesses immortality and dwells in unapproachable light" (1 Timothy 6:15-16).**

The term **"unapproachable light"** is about God's full glory. The glory of God is a very distinct characteristic of the eternal city. God's glory is so brilliant that the eternal city has no need for the light of the sun or moon. In Revelation 21:23 we read, **"And the city has no need of the sun or of the moon to shine on it, for the glory of God has illumined it, and its lamp is the Lamb."** The presence of God literally fills this city! It's no wonder the writer of Hebrews says of this city, **"the city which has foundations, whose architect and builder is God"** **(Hebrews 11:10).** The glory of God permeates every area of the city! God's glory will fill the eternal city as well as the new heavens and the new earth. John describes this light by calling our attention to its brilliance. He says, **"Her brilliance was like a very costly stone, as a stone crystal clear jasper."** The brilliance and splendor of the city is on display. The brilliance and splendor of God is on display! Because the words being used to describe the city are **"brilliance"** and **"crystal clear jasper"** they are in reference to a diamond. Diamonds are known for their brilliance! In this present earth, jasper is not crystal clear but an opaque usually red stone. In other words, the eternal city looks like one gigantic diamond! Only this diamond has no flaws or imperfections! The city resembles something that we've never seen, a perfect, flawless, crystal clear diamond that refracts and reflects the light of the glory of God! The eternal city is like a flawless diamond with light shining from within its brilliance. What a magnificent city! This city is stunningly beautiful! This city is stunningly brilliant! Are you longing to get there? I am. The new Jerusalem will serve as the focal point of life in eternity.

I'm sure you've heard the saying that some Christ followers are "so heavenly minded that they're no earthly good." As Christ followers and according to the Scriptures, we should all be **MORE** heavenly minded, not less! God has prepared an incomparable city, one that's without equal in which we will live for eternity, yet we almost never talk about it. We're more earthly good if we were more heavenly minded! I'm reminded of the words spoken by apostle Paul, "Therefore if you have been raised up with Christ, **KEEP SEEKING THE THINGS ABOVE,** where Christ is, seated at the right hand of God. **SET YOUR MIND ON THINGS ABOVE,** not on the things that are on earth" (Colossians 3:1-2). It really doesn't get any clearer than that! We're encouraged to be "heavenly minded!"

Chapter Twelve: God's Amazing Grace and Mercy (Revelation 7: 9-17)

In another part of this book, we talked about the 144,000 bond servants of the Lord. We talked about their salvation, identification, and divine protection for service during the tribulation. All this information is covered in Revelation 7:1-8. We learned that the 5th seal was a revelation concerning the martyrs who had been slain for their faith in Christ Jesus. We learned that the tribulation will begin with only unbelievers since the church has been taken away through the rapture and kept from this "hour of trial." Considering this, the question is, "How do people come to faith in the Lord during the tribulation?" We find the answer to this question in this study of God's amazing grace and mercy! Before we continue, let's define the words "grace" and "mercy." Grace gives, mercy withholds! In other words, grace "gives what is not deserved." Mercy "withholds what is deserved." The grace of God gives salvation, which is not deserved. Mercy withholds the verdict of guilty and the penalty that verdict demands, which all deserved because of sin. Because of their salvation, identification, protection and service to God, the 144,000 Jews become the evangelists of the tribulation. This speaks of the grace and mercy of God. Revelation 14:4 declares that the 144,000 are "the ones who follow the Lamb wherever He goes. They have been purchased from among men as first fruits to God and the Lamb." In other words, the 144,000 represent the first installment of a much larger group of salvations!

"After these things I looked, and behold, a great multitude which no one could count, from every nation and all tribes and peoples and tongues, standing before the throne and before the Lamb, clothed in white robes,

and palm branches were in their hands" (Revelation 7:9).

Let's examine this passage. The words of John are describing the greatest movement of God's saving power (in terms of total numbers) the world has ever known. This is wonderful news! God's grace and mercy are astonishing! God is a saving God. The phrase **"after these things"** is about the salvation, identification, and divine protection for service of the 144,000 Jews **(Revelation 7:1-8).** Apostle John looked in amazement and saw another wonderful sight. He saw a **"great multitude which no one could count."** In the amazing plan of God for Israel, He uses the Jewish nation as instruments to lead a great multitude to salvation! Unlike the 144,000, there's no number given, only that **"which no one could count."** John uses the word **"Behold."** The term means, "To look upon in amazement." The amazement is that in such a time as this, the tribulation, the grace and mercy of God is equally manifest and made available. God will save many souls during this time of judgment. We must keep in mind that the tribulation is the time of God's determined wrath as the Lamb is breaking the seals and releasing catastrophic judgments that destroy men and women.

The tribulation is a time of war, famine, disease, earthquakes, etc. that will kill billions of people. However, during all of this, we still behold God saving people in a way to an extent not known before. It's no wonder that John looked upon this great multitude with amazement! John tells us that this multitude is **"from every nation and all tribes and peoples and tongues."** John has told us that the 144,000 were all Jewish men, but this multitude is composed of all nationalities. This multitude will include Jews that are saved beyond the 144,000. John sees this multitude **"standing before the throne and before the**

Lamb." Revelation 7:15 also mentions that this multitude is **"before the throne of God."** This throne is the same one that's mentioned in chapters 4 and 5 of Revelation and reveals that they're in heaven in the presence of the Lamb of God as redeemed, blood-bought people. The phrase, **"standing before the throne and before the Lamb"** describes positions of honor and privilege. This multitude of martyred tribulation believers are now in the presence of God and the Lamb. They have come out of the great tribulation by way of being put to death for their belief in Christ. Death for the tribulation saints, as well as with the church saints, means to be in the presence of the Lord. Paul said it best with these words, "...**we are of good courage, I say, and prefer rather to be absent from the body and to be at home with the Lord" (2 Corinthians 5:8).**

Being absent from the body refers to the death of the believer, in which the person separates from his body to go into the presence of the Lord. Notice that death is not an obliteration of the person as some teach, but the person continues to exist with all their faculties in check. For those who are in Christ, death is a conscious state where we'll be still concerned about being in the presence of God. Now John tells us about their spiritual condition with these words, **"clothed in white robes."** This phrase speaks of the imputed righteousness of Jesus that was given to them at salvation. This phrase means that they're in Christ and have His righteousness as all who are considered justified before God (see Romans 3:24-26). Verses 14 and 15 of Revelation chapter 7 reveals that being **"clothed in white robes"** is the reason that this multitude has access to the throne and God's presence. **"And palm branches were in their hands."** In ancient times, palm branches were associated with worship and joyous celebrations, including the Feast of Tabernacles (Leviticus 23:40; John 12:12-13).

"And they cry out with a loud voice, saying 'Salvation to our God who sits on the throne, and to the Lamb.' And all the angels were standing around the throne and around the elders and the four living creatures; and they fell on their faces before the throne and worshiped God saying, Amen, blessing and glory and wisdom and thanksgiving and honor and power and might, be to our God forever and ever, Amen" (Revelation 7:10-12).

They are proclaiming that salvation belongs to God. Salvation is the theme of their praise and worship. God alone is the source of salvation (John 14:6; Acts 4:12). For the Christ follower, there's not a better reason to praise and worship God! They're engaged in praise that's very similar to the scene given in Revelation 5:8 (chapter 3 of this book). **"…all the angels were standing around the throne."** The mention of these angels is noteworthy. This is because God's holy angels have always been fascinated by God's redeeming power. First Peter 1:12 teaches that angels have always wanted to glimpse into these things pertaining to salvation. Apostle Paul tells us that God redeems the church to put His manifold wisdom on display before **"the rulers and the authorities in the heavenly places" (Ephesians 3:8-11).** Angels are continually involved in the worship of God's person and work. The 24 elders who represent the raptured church, are there singing and praising God for their salvation. Notice that salvation is to our **"God who sits on the throne."** That is a remarkable phrase. Apostle John actually saw God sitting on the throne! The word "sitting" describes the position of a king who is actively reigning. For example, if a politician is "seated," he is said to be in office. If a politician is put out of office, he is said to be "unseated." John sees God "seated," meaning He is actively exercising His sovereignty, ruling over the affairs of His creation.

Have you ever asked yourself the question: where is God in all of this? If you have, you're not alone! It's easy to want to ask this question every time you watch the evening news or read the newspaper. This world is sinking deeper and deeper into a quagmire of sin, while the Christian community seems to be on the short end of the stick. The church appears to be making less of an impact on our culture, not more. It's easy to ask, "God are You still in control?" As we see our world falling apart all around us we must be reminded that God is doing something. He has not resigned. There are no term limits to His being God! Have you looked up lately to see God still upon His throne? Have you come to understand that His sovereign throne controls the events of your life? **No matter what may seem out of control in your life, know that God is always in control!** God who sits on the throne is actively engaged in ruling over His creation as well as bringing a great multitude to Jesus Christ. Remember these words of Jesus, **"For this reason I have said to you, that no one can come to Me unless it has been granted him from the Father" (John 6:65).**

"Then one of the elders answered, saying to me, "These who are clothed in the white robes, who are they, and where have they come from?" I said to him, "My lord, you know." And he said to me, "These are the ones who come out of the great tribulation, and they have washed their robes and made them white in the blood of the Lamb" (Revelation 7:13-14).

Apostle John being puzzled as to the identity of this great multitude is asked the question, **"who are they, and where have they come from?"** Now John's answer comes with these words, **"These are the ones who come out of the great tribulation."** Let's examine the phrase **"who come out."** This phrase is present tense and continuous. In other words, this phrase shows a prolonged process and is translated, **"the ones coming out."** This multitude continues to accumulate as people keep being martyred! Remember in our teaching concerning **"An Examination of the Six Seals," we covered these tribulation martyrs (Revelation 6:9-11).** They asked the Lord how long would He hold off from revenging their deaths at the hands of those who dwell on the earth. Our Lord's answer to these martyrs was, **"until the number of their fellow servants and brethren who were to be killed even as they had been, would be completed also."** That statement from the Lord is in reference to, **"These are the ones who come out of the great tribulation."** Their number was still in the process of being completed! This martyred group continues to accumulate. What an awesome display of God's grace and mercy! This multitude comes about through a continual process of people coming out and coming out over the years of the tribulation. Any person who loves souls is going to have to rejoice in this because the beast and the false prophet are doing their best, trying to destroy the work of Jesus Christ, and God is pouring out His wrath as the Lamb breaks the seals. However, during all of this, God is saving souls and they keep coming out, they keep coming out, they keep coming out! Praise God forevermore! Thank God for His grace and mercy! The phrase, "they keep coming out" is descriptive of God's grace and mercy!

John says, **"they have washed their robes and made them white in the blood of the Lamb."** The emphasis is on the blood of the Lamb! Regular blood doesn't get anything clean! It stains and must be cleaned. But the blood of Jesus doesn't stain! It cleanses every stain of sin. The blood of the Lamb removes sin altogether. The topic of the blood of the Lamb is throughout the Revelation of Jesus Christ. In Revelation 1:5, we read, **"To Him who**

loves us and released us from our sins by His blood."
Revelation 5:9 states, **"You purchased for God with
Your blood men from every tribe and tongue and
people and nation."** Revelation 12:11 states, **"And they
overcame him because of the blood of the Lamb and
because of the word of their testimony, and they did not
love their life even when faced with death."** Since we are
here at Revelation 12:11, let's take a closer look at what it
teaches. The context of this passage takes us back to
Revelation 12:7. **"And there was war in heaven, Michael
and his angels waging war with the dragon. The dragon
and his angels waged war, and they were not strong
enough, and there was no longer a place found for them
in heaven" (v7).** John informs us that there was war in
heaven. This is a future war that will be waged during the
tribulation period as verse 12 explains. John explains that,
"they were not strong enough." The dragon and his
angels were not strong enough to defeat Michael and his
angels. Because they were not strong enough, we're given
this result: **"and there was no longer a place found for
them in heaven."**

Presently, Satan has access to heaven to accuse the brethren
(Job 1:6-7; 2:1-2; Zechariah 3:1-2). However, now, access
will be denied! Understand that this battle is not between
God and Satan, but between Satan and Michael. Satan
could not win against Michael; how can he ever win against
God? Never forget that Satan is a created being and is not
equal to God. Satan is **NO MATCH FOR GOD!**
Michael's name means **"one who is like God."** In Jude
1:9, Michael is called **"the archangel."** Here we're told
that the one who is like God defeats the one who wants to
be God! John shares, **"And the great dragon was thrown
down, the serpent of old who is called the devil and
Satan, who deceives the whole world; he was thrown
down to the earth, and his angels were thrown down**

with him" (v 9). Notice that Satan is called one "who deceives the whole world." This emphasizes the character and activity of Satan. He is the deceiver. This word "deceives" means "to lead astray, mislead, to cause one to believe a lie for the truth." His deceptions are what causes people to miss the truth of God. He has many strategies for deception:

1. He's a liar! Not only is he a liar, but all lying originated with him! That's why the Lord called him "a liar and the father of lies" (John 8:44).
2. He denies the truth (1 John 4:3; 2 Peter 2:2).
3. He perverts the truth (1 Timothy 4:1-5; Galatians 3:1-3).

John shares that Satan and his angels will be "thrown down to the earth." In other words, the accusing, slandering activities of Satan against believers in Christ is over! The time of his judgment is at hand. In verse 10, John shares "Then I heard a loud voice in heaven, saying, 'Now the salvation, and the power, and the kingdom of our God and the authority of His Christ have come, for the accuser of our brethren has been thrown down, he who accuses them before our God day and night'" (Revelation 12:10). John wants us to understand that Satan's accusations against the brethren are really attempts to distort and attack as being false the character of God. But apostle Paul teaches us that the wisdom of God's plan allowed Him to punish Christ in the place of sinners and thereby justify those who are guilty without compromising His character. Paul said, "For the demonstration, of His righteousness at the present time, so that He would be just and the justifier of the one who has faith in Jesus" (Romans 3:26).

"And they overcame him because of the blood of the Lamb and because of the word of their testimony, and they did not love their life even when faced with death" (v 11). This passage teaches us how the tribulation saints will overcome Satan and his onslaughts. John says, **"They overcame him by the blood of the Lamb."** The phrase **"the blood of the Lamb"** is in reference to the person and work of Jesus on the cross. The cross of Christ is the place and the means of the devil's defeat (John 16:8; Colossians 2:15; Hebrews 2:14). It was at the cross where Christ answered all accusations of Satan proving that God is perfectly consistent with His divine being. The cross demonstrated that He is just and the justifier of the one who has faith in Jesus! Because of the blood of the Lamb, we can always stand against and overcome the devil. John shares, **"And because of the word of their testimony."** What is the activity that overcomes and defeats the devil? It's the proclamation of the Word of God, sound biblical teaching, and the truth concerning Christ both by **WORDS AND LIFESTYLE!** By biblical words that lineup with our lifestyles; Christ followers can nullify the accusations of Satan as well as expose him for the liar that he is. In heaven, we have an Advocate, the Lord Jesus Christ, who counters Satan's accusations, and we are to answer his accusations based on consistent godly living here on earth. The world claims that man does not need God, but we can show that the world is in error when we don't live as the world lives. John shares, **"And they did not love their life even when face with death."** Here we're given the attitude which enables us to overcome the devil. This phrase is very powerful and needs to be understood and embraced.

There is the point of view of living considering eternity by seeing this life as a vapor and temporary. This will lead us to the next attitude necessary to overcome Satan. It's the attitude of unswerving faith even in the face of death, because we know that this life is not the end. Paul tells us, **"If we have hoped in Christ in this life only, we are of all men most to be pitied" (1 Corinthians 15:19).** We have a life and an inheritance in Christ that's not touched by death in this life! Praise the Lord forevermore!

Chapter 13: Rewards and the Christ Follower (the judgment seat of Christ)

Let's take a brief survey of what the Scriptures have to say regarding rewards for faithfulness to the Lord Jesus Christ. **Romans 14:10 says, "But you, why do you judge your brother? Or you again, why do you regard your brother with contempt? For we will all stand before the judgment seat of God." 1 Corinthians 3:11-15 says, "For no man can lay a foundation other than the one which is laid, which is Jesus Christ. Now if any man builds on the foundation with gold, silver, precious stones, wood, hay, straw, each man's work will become evident; for the day will show it because it is to be revealed with fire, and the fire itself will test the quality of each man's work. If any man's work which he has built on it remains, he will receive a reward. If any man's work is burned up, he will suffer loss; but he himself will be saved, yet so as through fire."**

Also, Paul reminds us, **"Therefore we also have as our ambition, whether at home or absent, to be pleasing to Him. For we must all appear before the judgment of Christ, so that each one may be recompensed for his deeds in the body, according to what he has done, whether good or bad" (2 Corinthians 5:9-10). Revelation 22:12 says, "Behold, I am coming quickly, and My reward is with Me, to render to every man according to what he has done."**

In **Hebrews 11:6,** we read, **"And without faith it is impossible to please Him, for he who comes to God must believe that He is and that He is a rewarder of**

those who seek Him." Though the context of Hebrews 11 shows that God rewards the faith that we put in Him with forgiveness and justification, it still speaks to the fact that God is a rewarder! Rewards are a part of the plan and purpose of God for the Christ follower. It's just not possible to read the Scriptures without coming face to face with the truth that God is a rewarder of the Christ follower. Having said that, I hope that you will see the importance of the topic of rewards for the Christ follower!

Before we continue, let me say that the judgment seat of Christ is not a judgment of condemnation. Apostle Paul assures the Christ follower that, **"Therefore there is now no condemnation for those who are in Christ Jesus" (Romans 8:1).** That's very good news! The Greek word translated "condemnation" is about a guilty verdict and the penalty that verdict demands. Jesus said it this way, **"Truly, truly, I say to you, he who hears My words, and believes Him who sent Me, has eternal life, and does not come into judgment, but has passed out of death into life" (John 5:24).** In other words, Christ followers will never be condemned! The judgment of condemnation is covered in another place of this book (the great white throne judgment).

When does the judgment seat of Christ take place? Let's examine these passages and what they teach about the rewards of all who live lives of faithfulness to Christ. The Greek word translated "reward" means, "Something paid back," or "payment for something done." We see God doing this throughout the New Testament in all the passages that were mentioned. This event will happen after the resurrection and removal of the church from the earth. The resurrection and removal (rapture) of the church is explained in 1 Thessalonians 4:11-13. It's also covered in detail in this book. A careful reading of the passage in 2 Corinthians 5:9-10, reveals the context as that of our earthly and heavenly existence (2 Corinthians 5:6-8). This passage leads to the conclusion that this event will happen in heaven after the rapture of the church.

A Look At Romans 14:10

It reads, **"But you, why do you judge your brother? Or you again, why do you regard your brother with contempt? For we will all stand before the judgment seat of God" (Romans 14:10).** We must understand that apostle Paul is not against all judgment! He is not condemning all judgment. Paul is teaching against judging others on matters where Scripture has no commands for judging! This teaching is found within the context of Paul's statement in **Romans 14:10, "why do you judge your brother?"** The context of Paul's statement takes us back to Romans 14:5, where he says, **"One person regards one day above another, another regards every day alike. Each person must be fully convinced in his own mind."** In other words, each Christ follower must follow his or her own conscience **with respect to matters not specifically commanded or prohibited in God's Word!** This is what Paul was dealing with when he said the words of **Romans 14:10, "why do you judge your brother?"** This is what the apostle means with the words, **"Each person must be fully convinced in his own mind" (Romans 14:5).** Clearly, Paul would not have said, "Each person must be fully convinced in his own mind" about whether committing adultery was wrong. Paul would not have said, "One person has no problem with committing adultery, whereas another person has a problem with it, so each person must be fully convinced in his own mind." Paul would not have said, "Each person must be fully convinced in his own mind" about whether homosexuality was wrong. Paul would not have said, "One person has no problem with committing homosexual acts, whereas another person has a problem with it, so each person must be fully convinced in his own mind." Every Christ follower knows that these two acts are prohibited by God in Scripture! These acts as well as others prohibited by God must be judged!! As a matter of fact, Paul rebuked and admonished the church at Corinth because they did not judge a brother for his immoral actions (1 Corinthians 5:1-5)!

We are right to judge one another over matters of sin or errors in doctrine. In the **Romans 14:10 passage, Paul shares, "For we will all stand before the judgment seat of God."** However, in his letter to the Corinthians, he says, **"For we must all appear before the judgment seat of Christ" (2 Corinthians 5:10).** According to John 10:30, Christ said, "I and the Father are one." In other words, since Jesus and God are one, Paul in both passages is speaking about the same judgment seat. Maybe you're thinking, "How can a person have his or her sins forgiven and still have their works examined at the judgment seat of God?" We must understand and embrace that God's forgiveness of us is about being justified, but our rewards are about the works we've done as people who have been justified (made right before God)!

What Happens at the Judgment Seat?

To find the answer, let's turn to the passage of **2 Corinthians 5:9-10.** It reads, **"Therefore we also have as our ambition, whether at home or absent, to be pleasing** to Him. **For we must all appear before the judgment seat of Christ, so that each one may be recompensed for his deeds in the body, according to what he has done whether good or bad."** What an awesome assurance we have with the phrase, **"whether at home or absent."** This phrase takes us back to verses 6-8. While the Christ follower is alive on earth (at home in the body), he is absent from the Lord (the fullness of the presence of God). Whether we're in our present bodies or with the Lord in heaven, our living to please the Lord remains! In other words, we have no excuse for not being careful about how we're living now because our bodies will perish, but the deeds done while in these bodies will be examined at the judgment seat of Christ!

Paul says, **"we also have as our ambition."** What does he mean? Paul is clearly speaking about his ambition in life. What was Paul's ambition in life? Should it be our ambition as well? The Greek word translated "ambition" means "to love what is honorable." As a Christ follower, how would your life change if that was your ambition? As Christ followers, we are to be diligent in going after all that's honorable before Christ Jesus! Paul uses the phrase **"pleasing to Him."** Loving what's honorable is pleasing to Christ! As Christ followers, we are to be passionate about living to please the Lord!

The following is an excerpt from The MacArthur New Testament Commentary on 2 Corinthians 5.

> "Driving Paul's noble ambition was the knowledge that there would be a penetrating uncovering of the depths of his heart by the Lord Himself. That will take place in the future when believers must all appear before the judgment seat of Christ. The strong terms must and all stress the inevitability and

comprehensiveness of this event. That knowledge produced in Paul strong motivation to please God in this life. In that day, the full truth about their lives, character, and deeds will be made clear to each believer. Each will discover the real verdict on his or her ministry, service, and motives. All hypocrisy and pretense will be stripped away; all temporal matters with no eternal significance will vanish like wood, hay, and stubble, and only what is to be rewarded as eternally valuable will be left."

This writer agrees with John MacArthur. Kenneth Boa says,

"There's going to be a day of reckoning. The Lord who gives great gifts will also return to settle accounts (see Matthew 25:19). This is going to be a performance review that will make every other performance review you've ever received seem inconsequential. We may be able to lip-sync our way through life, but we'll all sing a cappella in front of God. This should serve as a wake-up call for complacent Christians. We must not allow ourselves to be seduced by the things this world deems important. Most of what the world tells us to pursue is related to the opinions of others, but at the judgment seat of Christ, their opinions will be irrelevant. Only his opinion will matter."

This writer agrees with Kenneth Boa. Understanding and embracing the biblical teaching about rewards will help to move us out of being complacent! Sometimes we need a "kick in our complacency!" The time for preparing for the judgment seat of Christ is now! Let me encourage you to begin living for eternity right now. Let me encourage you to begin living with an eye toward appearing at the judgment seat of Christ! According to Apostle Paul, living this way was linked to his ambition in life (2 Corinthians 5:9-10). We're one day closer to eternity than we were yesterday! It's the wisdom of God for us to prepare to meet Christ at the judgment seat. Paul says, **"according to what he has done whether good or bad."** Again, since this judgment is not for sin, the words "good" and "bad" are about that which will last (good), and that which is not good or useless (bad). This is spelled out more clearly in our next passage.

A Look at 1 Corinthians 3:10-15

Paul says, **"According to the grace of God which was given to me, like a wise master builder I laid a foundation, and another is building on it. But each man must be careful how he builds on it. For no man can lay a foundation other than the one which is laid, which is Jesus Christ. Now if any man builds on the foundation with gold, silver, precious stones, wood, hay, straw, each man's work will become evident; for the day will show it because it is to be revealed with fire, and the fire itself will test the quality of each man's work. If any man's work which he has built on it remains, he will receive a reward. If any man's work is burned up, he will suffer loss; but he himself will be saved, yet as through fire."**

Paul identifies himself as **"a wise master builder."** What does this mean? In speaking about spiritual rewards, Paul uses the language of an architect and designer of buildings. In other words, Paul is using the language of construction to teach about the rewards of the Christ follower! Paul's emphasis is on careful building! He tells us, **"I laid a foundation."** Any building that's going to stand must be carefully built on a solid foundation. Any good architect will tell you that the foundation is the most important part of a building, for it must be solid to withstand the changing elements, support the weight of the structure, and endure for a long time.

The church of Jesus Christ has been constructed on the solid foundation of Jesus Christ! As a wise master builder, Paul laid the foundation of the church in Corinth. Paul is emphasizing this: As we build our lives, let's not lose the focus of our foundation! He says, **"But each man must be careful how he builds on it."** Next, the master builder must build with quality materials. This is because he's building for eternity! The question is "What are we building with?"

The materials are listed as **"gold, silver, precious stones, wood, hay, straw."** Gold, silver, and precious stones are symbolic of things that have lasting value. Wood, hay, and straw are just the opposite. We have superior materials (gold, silver, and precious stones) contrasted with inferior materials (wood, hay, and straw). Paul says, **"Each man's work will become evident."** What does he mean? It means the building will be examined to show what kind of material was used. This happens at the judgment seat of Christ. Paul says, **"The fire itself will test the quality of each man's work."** The fire will reveal whether our works have any value. The materials are either permanent or temporary. The choice is ours! Fire purifies gold, silver, and precious stones, but consumes wood, hay, and straw. Only what we do in obedience to Christ will last!

Why all the concern that we build carefully and with the right materials? Paul answers with these words, **"If any man's work which he has built on it remains, he will receive a reward."** As Christ followers, we'll receive rewards at the judgment seat of Christ for works that bring glory, honor, and pleasure to God! Let's begin building today for eternity!

Epilogue (Revelation 22:6-21)

A look at the concluding promises of the prophecy
(Revelation 22:6-16)

Let's examine the importance of the awesome words of this epilogue. The verses of this epilogue contain the testimony of the angel, Christ, the Holy Spirit, the bride, and apostle John. These verses are significant in that they're full of encouragement, edification, comfort, warning, and response to God. Let's read them with care and attentiveness. Let's examine these words in terms of your whole life, your lifestyle, priorities and commitment to God, the Bible, and the soon coming Christ.

"And he said to me, "These words are faithful and true" and the Lord, the God of the spirits of the prophets, sent His angel to show to His bond servants the things which must soon take place" (Revelation 22:6).

"And he said to me, These words are faithful and true." (Revelation 22:6).

What comes to mind is the fact that God's words are certain and completely reliable. Literally the Greek reads, **"these words (the entire revelation), faithful and true."** In other words, the Greek rendering emphasizes the ideas of faithful and true. **"Faithful"** means reliable, trustworthy. **"True"** means real, genuine, as opposed to false. What an awesome privilege it is to feed on the faithfulness of God! The benefits are out of this world! Feeding on God's faithfulness enables us to grow, develop, and mature in our relationship with God, through Christ Jesus! The Words of God stand in stark contrast to the human viewpoint that many try to build their lives on. Man's viewpoint apart from God's perspective can only be built upon the limitations of human wisdom, reason and experience. Because of sin, man's viewpoint is not reliable, especially with respect to spiritual concerns. The issue for us here and throughout Scripture is that which makes the Word of God faithful and true. We see that behind **"these words"** is **"the Lord, the God of the spirits of the prophets." "Lord"** is synonymous for God's sovereignty, complete authority, and power. **"God"** emphasizes the aspect of God's divine nature as God. This contrasts with man and the human viewpoint. In other words, all that God is stands behind **"these words."** A name is that by which a person or thing is known. Christ is known by the name **"Faithful and True" (Revelation 19:11).** Praise the Lord forevermore! It's a very refreshing thing to take God at His Word. It's a very refreshing thing to believe God simply because He said it! Praise God forevermore!

"And behold, I am coming quickly. Blessed is he who heeds the words of the prophecy of this book" (Revelation 22:7).

Here we're given the promise of the Lord's coming. John says, **"behold, I am coming quickly."** This is an event which must come to pass! This is about the Lord's return to rapture the church from the earth. Once again, we see the blessed hope of the Christ follower, which is the rapture of the church that keeps us out of the hour of trial, the tribulation (Revelation 3:10). This is covered in detail in another chapter of this book. Let's consider some things here about this promise. We'll start with the word **"behold."** It means to look upon with amazement, to arouse attention. **The promise that Christ our Redeemer is coming for us should arouse our attention and cause**

us to be amazed. What an awesome event this will be in our lives. Next, we see the phrase **"I am coming."** Our Lord's return for us is assured. It's already in the process of coming to pass. Then we see the word **"quickly."** This word means "speedy, at once, or suddenly." The point is that our Lord's coming to rapture the church is imminent. It could happen at any moment! This is covered in detail in chapter six. Next, we're given the pronouncement of blessing on those who obey the Word of God. Joy or being blessed is always connected with the obedience to God's revealed Words. This wonderful passage describes the blessing or joy which comes from facing life and its many problems with the promises of the Word of God. The word **"blessed"** is the Greek word which means "happy." It's not describing the fun and games happiness that the world gives, but the joy and contentment that only comes from trusting God by doing what His Word says.

Apostle James reminds us that it's the doer of God's Word that's **"blessed in what he does" (James 1:25).** Who are the recipients of this awesome promise? The passage says **"he who heeds."** This phrase speaks of the person who is consistent in the keeping of God's Word. The word **"heed"** is defined as "to guard, protect, watch over, keep in custody, and pay attention to." The idea is the personal application of God's Word. John says that we are to heed **"the words of the prophecy of this book."** We do this by keeping the words of the prophecy of this book **IN CUSTODY.** We learn it through accurate teaching and careful study. We **PAY ATTENTION TO IT** to obey it, and we **GUARD** what we've learned by keeping our minds renewed. The person who does these things will be blessed! There's simply no doubt about it! We have God's Word on it!

"I, John, am the one who heard and saw these things. And when I heard and saw, I fell down to worship at the feet of the angel who showed me these things. But he said to me, "Do not do that. I am a fellow servant of yours and of your brethren the prophets and of those who heed the words of this book. Worship God" (Revelation 22:8-9).

With the phrase **"I, John, am the one who heard and saw these things,"** John wants his readers to be encouraged and impressed with the fact that he really did hear and see these things. John is talking about the awesome things of the eternal city, the new Jerusalem, the city who's architect and builder is God! **The Greek text reads "the one hearing and seeing these things."** This is the present tense. The visions that John had were at that point a past fact. But John used the present tense to stress the importance of the reality of these visions he'd received. John says, **"I fell down to worship at the feet of the angel."** Can you imagine the wonder and excitement that had taken hold of John? In the process of seeing and hearing these things, John, in error, worships the messenger.

We saw this same thing happen in Revelation 19:10. It's repeated for our learning. The message of the Word of God is intended for the Christ follower to focus on the Lord and make better our worship of Him, and we're never to lose sight of that. The angel recognizes this fact and corrects John with the words, **"Do not do that."** The angel is emphasizing that only God is deserving of our worship and adoration. I'm reminded of these words, **"Worthy are You, our Lord and our God, to receive glory and honor and power; for You created all things, and because of Your will they existed, and were created"** (Revelation 4:11). God who is the Creator of all things, including what

John saw and heard, is the only One deserving our worship. Praise God forevermore!

"Behold, I am coming quickly, and My reward is with Me, to render to every man according to what he has done" (Revelation 22:12).
These words are designed to encourage us to godly living in this present time. The life we live today is a preparation time for life in eternity. This is a significant reason for us to live now with a view toward eternity. There are rewards at stake in the eternal state. There are positions of responsibility at stake. We all must be reminded of why the Bible calls us **"strangers and foreigners" in this life (Hebrews 11:13).** We're just passing through this life to the life in the eternal state. One day we're going to be with Jesus and the way we live right now will determine how we reign with Jesus in eternity. Let's continue to be "heavenly minded!" With the words, **"I am coming quickly"** the Lord reminds us that His coming for His church is imminent! This passage declares the suddenness of His return.

"I am the Alpha and the Omega, the first and the last, the beginning and the end" (Revelation 22:13).

This passage emphasizes the eternal nature of Christ. The phrase **"I am the Alpha and the Omega"** is used at the start of the revelation of Jesus (Revelation 1:8), and here at the epilogue of the revelation of Jesus. Why? The words **"Alpha and Omega"** are the first and last words of the Greek alphabet. They are in reference to the extent of our Lord's knowledge, wisdom, and understanding! **The usage of "Alpha and Omega" validates the communication of the entire Revelation of Jesus Christ!**

"Blessed are those who wash their robes, so that they may have the right to the tree of life, and may enter by the gates into the city. Outside are the dogs and sorcerers and the immoral persons and the murderers and the idolaters, and everyone who loves and practices lying" (Revelation 22:14-15).

This passage contains the promise of blessing to **"those who wash their robes."** What does this mean?

The robe symbolizes a person's condition of being right with God. It is the condition of righteousness. This phrase is symbolic of all who have been forgiven by God through the precious blood of Christ, the Lamb of God! The word **"right"** in the phrase **"that they may have the right"** is both the authority to do something as well as the power to do something. There is a difference between power and authority! Christ followers have the righteousness of God credited to them (Romans 4:22-25; 2 Corinthians 5:21). **Because of righteousness being credited and the body being glorified, the Christ follower will have both the authority and the ability to live in the eternal city where righteousness dwells!** Apostle Peter says, **"But according to His promise we are looking for new heavens and a new earth, in which righteousness dwells" (2 Peter 3:13). The reason we're to look for "new heavens and a new earth in which righteousness dwells," is because we have been made "the righteousness of God in Him" (2 Corinthians 5:21).** Being made the righteousness of God in Christ is what happens to every person who has faith in the finished work of Christ on the cross. Is this true of you? If not, it can be if you'd believe that Jesus took your place on that cross. We're given a contrast of those who have access to the city and those who are not given access. Notice that the words used for all those who do not believe describes the character that these people are left with. They do not have the righteousness of God credited to them so they must continue in their sin as **"the dogs and sorcerers and the immoral persons and the murderers and the idolaters, and everyone who loves and practices lying."**

Jesus said it best with these words, **"Therefore I said to you that you will die in your sins; for unless you believe that I am He, you will die in your sins." (John 8:24).** The people listed in Revelation 22:15 are the people that Jesus was speaking about in John 8:24. What I'm stressing is, this does not have to describe you! You can believe on Jesus as your Lord and Savior! The people listed in Revelation 22:15 are showing us our need for a Savior. His name is Jesus! **Not only are these who are listed in verse 15 excluded from the eternal city, but they will continue throughout eternity in the misery and sorrow of their fallen, sinful state.** For me personally, one of the things that I'm really looking forward to is being released from my sinful nature. Apostle Paul said it best with these words, **"For I know that nothing good dwells in me, that is, in my flesh; for the willing is present in me, but the doing of the good is not. For the good that I want, I do not do, but I practice the very evil that I do not want. But if I am doing the very thing I do not want, I am no longer the one doing it, but sin which dwells in me"** **(Romans 7:18-20).** I'm looking forward to my complete and permanent change that comes from having a glorified body, one with no sin nature! I'm looking forward to getting rid of the **"sin which dwells in me."** Praise God!

"I, Jesus, have sent My angel to testify to you these things for the churches. I am the root and the descendant of David, the bright morning star" (Revelation 22:16).

Take note of the fact that in this verse, we have the first mention of the word "church," the "called out ones," since Revelation chapter 3. This shows that the church is not in the tribulation as some believe. Recall that Revelation chapters 6-19, which cover the tribulation, also deals with Israel. For this and other reasons the church is not present or talked about. This is covered in detail in another part of the book. The Lord Jesus is giving us assurance of these things by the words **"I am the root and descendant of David, the bright morning star."** What does this mean? The phrase **"I am the root and the descendant of David"** is about the passage in Isaiah 11:1, where it's said that from Jesse, the future King of the entire earth, would rise up like a shoot from the root of a cut down tree. We know that the Davidic line would be cut down so that no man would occupy the throne of David (Jeremiah 22:24-30), **but from David's roots would come Messiah. Christ who came after David as his offspring was also before David as the root! Only Jesus can be David's descendant as well as David's Creator! Christ as the root and descendant of David will restore the people of Israel to the place of promised blessing.** Apostle Paul speaks of this in Romans 11. Jesus also calls Himself **"the bright morning star."** Literally the Greek text reads **"the star, the bright one, the morning one."** What is significant about a morning star? It brings confidence of a new day and the end of the night. Christ as the morning star proclaims and gives assurance to us of the ending of this present night time and the coming of a new day that happens when He removes the church from the earth which sets in motion all that's promised to follow!

"I testify to everyone who hears the words of the prophecy of this book: if anyone adds to them, God will add to him the plagues which are written in this book; and if anyone takes away from the words of the book of

this prophecy, God will take away his part from the tree of life and from the holy city, which are written in this book" (Revelation 22:18-19).

The phrase **"to everyone who hears"** has been emphasized in the entire book of Revelation (2:7, 11, 17, 29; 3:6, 13, 20, 22). Because of the emphasis of this phrase the question becomes "are you knowing the truth about God?" Are you hearing the truth about God? The way that God has revealed Himself to us is through the Scriptures. Because of this truth, all are without excuse. If we choose any other way of trying to know God, we will not hear from Him. God is not revealing Himself in any other way. God can be known. This knowledge of God comes only through His Word. Jesus said, **"And you shall know the truth, and the truth will make you free" (John 8:32).** It's knowing the truth of the Bible which sets us free. So, we must have "ears to hear!" What does the phrase, **"God will take away his part from the tree of life and from the holy city"** mean? What it does not mean, as some believe, is that a person can lose salvation. The person that's saved will not tamper with the Bible! The saved person will not alter the Scripture. Anyone who alters the truth for any reason will incur the judgments which are described in this passage.

"He who testifies to these things says, "Yes, I am coming quickly." Amen. Come, Lord Jesus. The grace of the Lord Jesus be with all. Amen" (Revelation 22:20-21).

Here we're given the benediction. The imminent return of Christ for the church again is emphasized! Notice the word **"Amen."** This word means "the truth." The words **"I am coming quickly"** are followed by the word "Amen" which means "the truth!" The word **"quickly"** means "momentarily, at any moment!" Do you see what's being emphasized? Jesus is stressing the truth about Him coming quickly! John begins to pray in response to Jesus' words, **"I am coming quickly"** by saying, **"Come, Lord Jesus."** Praise God forevermore! What if the church got back to praying, "Come, Lord Jesus?" It would show a firm persuasion that Christ could return for the church at any moment!

About the Author

Robert Taylor is pastor of Teach Well Bible Church in Pikeville, North Carolina. His sound and practical teachings, through the pulpit, as well as www.TeachWellBibleChurch.org and www.TeachWellOnLine.org, reaches people both nationally and internationally. Pastor Robert's teaching ministry is committed to providing Christ followers with sound, wholesome Bible teaching that's relevant to our constantly changing society. His first book, **"The Future of Humanity: Racing Toward Eternity,"** is an outreach of his teaching ministry.